Playing out in the Wireless Days

Copyright © Michael Glover 2017

Cover photograph © the estate of Peter Owen-Jones
Photographs: Coningsby Rd © David Ainscough
www.copperbeechstudios.co.uk,
Sunbeam cinema © Mr J R Wrigley
The Star Walk © Sheffield Newspapers/The Star,
Grundig tape recorder courtesy of Hannes Grobe
hannes.grobe @awi.de,
The Gates of Heaven © Pete McKee. Top man!
(Thank you all)

Other pictures: the author or publisher

The chapter entitled 'Kitty's Routine' is an edited version of words extracted from Dorothy Glover's unpublished memoir.

www.1889books.co.uk

ISBN: 978-0-9935762-7-0

For Ruth, Jesse and Joseph

A Note About the Cover image

The cover image is taken from the painting *Terminus* by Peter Owen-Jones. Peter was born in the Peak District village of Bradwell in 1933, but moved to Sheffield where he studied a Diploma in Art and Illustration at Sheffield College of Art. He became Head of Art at King Edward VII School in the city, retiring at the age of 57 to devote his time to painting. Most of his works are in private ownership – sold at exhibitions or as commissions, including from British Rail and the Science Museum. He died in 1993 at the age of just 60. More of Peter's work can be seen, and prints purchased at:
http://www.peterowenjones.co.uk

Foreword

How far should we peer into the well of our own lives? That is the question I need to ask myself as I embark upon this sequel-of-sorts to my recent memoir, *Headlong into Pennilessness*. The first nineteen years of my life as described in that book, growing up as I did in the north-east end of Sheffield, were an age of relative innocence. In part, I was spoon-fed the truth by authorities greater than myself – my mother, my grandfather, my school, the Methodist Church to which I briefly pledged allegiance. I have written of that small terraced house in Fir Vale, north-east Sheffield where I grew up, with a tenderness bordering on innocence, if not naivety. There was a drabness, a smallness about life in that suburb of Sheffield in the 1950s, but it was the only life that I knew, and consequently it was fundamentally marvellous to the awakening senses of a small, world-ignorant child as only a young and relatively protected life can be marvellous.

I did not grow up in prosperity, but nor did I suffer poverty. There was always food on the table. There were always abundant gifts in the pillowcase on Christmas morning. There were always the fizzes and the shrieks of fireworks on Guy Fawkes Night. There was always the promise of that week at Mrs Ansell's boarding house in Blackpool, with its variety shows, its eating of fish and chips in the open air, its slot machines at the Olympia, and its sticks of rock from one of the shops on the Promenade to suck on or chomp at when they were unwrapped from their crackly cellophane...

And then there were books, and everything that books seemed to promise. In a time before regular transatlantic flights, books allowed you to take wing to imaginative elsewheres, to see, vividly, without necessarily being present in front of what you were seeing. The lure of the small, black-and-white television screen, with its regular, irritating zizz of visual interference, was as nothing beside the ever thickening and entirely uninterrupted appeal of books.

That was my world. And yet, I recognise now, that book was only a part of what I needed to say about the places and the people that I had lived amongst in those years. I discovered that simple fact when my nephew, the publisher of *Headlong Into Pennilessness*, asked me to think about a theme for a newspaper feature that might be published to coincide with a reading that I was due to give at Sheffield's annual Off the Shelf Festival. That event would be taking place at Firth Park Library, close to where I was born and went to school. That had been my library as a child and a growing man. I then quickly discovered that this was not quite the case. I was perjuring myself.

The library that I had known as Firth Park Library, the one that once huddled in beside the clock tower and the boating pond at the bottom end of the park, with its own turning circle for carriages in 1937, the year of its inauguration, had closed long ago. The new Firth Park Library – not so new by now – was in a different place altogether. It occupied a building formerly used by the Cooperative Society, at the top end of Firth Park. That is where my event would take place. When I discovered that fact, I experienced, all of a sudden, an acute sense of loss, and even a momentary and wholly irrational twinge of betrayal. The place that I knew and faithfully frequented in the 1950s and 1960s was no more.

I immediately suggested to Neil that I write some words about the old Firth Park Library, one of the local places that had nurtured me. This was a topic which I had not touched on in my memoir. After I had finished that piece, I began to discover that there were more and yet more places and people and incidents and objects in my early life that were perhaps worth rescuing from oblivion too. A new book would thicken out the story of my life, and also help to give a wider perspective upon this great city that I had grown up in. And, gradually, little by little, this book came into being.

There are many searching questions that arise during the writing of a book such as this one. To write of one's own life is, in the opinion of its author, to conjure up a world of near tedious familiarity. One knows one's own life too well. One has been too well versed in it for far too long. There are no particular surprises, no unanticipated climaxes or fearful disappointments. Everything that happened in it has already happened – to you.

And yet as soon as a book is published – as I discovered with *Headlong into Pennilessness* – quite different perspectives upon your own life hove into view. From the point of view of a man born in the South African veldt, for example, my early life was quite extraordinarily strange, if not exotic. The novelist Christopher Isherwood once told a story about his yearning, from a very early age, to visit the Equator. Could there be anything more wonderful than to stand at the very place where the world divides into two, the Northern Hemisphere above and the Southern Hemisphere below? Years later, as a grown man, he went there, and subsequently wrote about that experience in a book called *The Condor and the Cows*. The native equatorians were bewildered by his curiosity. Why ever would you want to come *here* of all places? they said to him. They would have preferred to see the marvels of London, New York – or perhaps Sheffield. Everyone's ordinariness is someone else's extraordinariness. In short, it is everything that they have not been and not lived through.

Here, spread out for your interest, like a scattering of cupcakes on a floral platter set on a rackety table in the old refreshment rooms of Firth Park Library, are some of the nooks and crannies of Sheffield that I first experienced, as child and growing man, many years ago.

At the Junction of Coningsby Road and Blyde Road, Fir Vale, Sheffield 5, 1965

This is the place where it all began for me: Coningsby Road, Fir Vale, Sheffield 5. It looks like any other nondescript northern street of late nineteenth-century, red-brick terraced housing, with a smearing of grey sky overhead, built for workers in the local steel industry. It never felt nondescript to me though. With its gennels leading, rather secretively, into individual asphalted back yards, each one shared by several families, and divided from its neighbour's by an almost (but not quite)-too-high-to-climb brick wall, it was everything I could ever have known and wished for in those days. Does that represent a poverty of ambition? Tell that to a child.

Just look at the condition of the road at this end! The tarmac has worn away to such a extent that you can see back to the original cobbles. And there were so few cars back then! In fact, that street was almost the private property of shouting and gostering kids – which meant ginger-haired Enid from the next yard, Clive Hacon from the beer-off on the corner, and me, for the most part. It was all about playing out in those days – running, tig, hopscotch; whooshing along on rackety bikes or scooters, or just lounging around against a low brick wall until it got dark enough to be called indoors for tea. I used to belt a football against that big gable end wall of the terrace on the left, as hard and as high as it would go. It never once bounced back so hard that it smashed a window. Say I. It broke some sweat though.

One of the best days I ever had in that street involved a miraculous discovery. I must have been about ten at the time. It happened just on the left of the picture, on that corner where a third car seems to be gently nosing its way out of the top end of Blyde Road. I can remember the spot to this day, just outside somebody's front door... I suddenly spotted a ten-pound note on the ground. It was a bit scruffy and crumpled, but it was still a ten pound note all right. I looked around, a bit furtively – there wasn't a soul in sight. I half-thought about knocking on that door, then thought better of it. Then I put it in my pocket, fast, and walked swoonily back up our gennel in a dream of riches. If I hadn't been so red in the face with excitement, I reckon that I wouldn't have had to own up to it to my mother.

In short, Coningsby Road was a perfectly marvellous place to grow up.

So marvellous, in fact, that, as you have already seen for yourself, at the head of this chapter, someone even thought to photograph it, as if it were a pin up on Blackpool Beach, in all its drab, day-to-day ingloriousness, about ten years before it was demolished to make way for a mad-cap scheme of road-widening that never in fact happened. The vision ran out. Or, more likely, the money ran out. Or got diverted in the direction of something a bit more pressing.

For years after that, Coningsby Road was nothing more than a sad strew of building rubble. All the people who had once lived there had been sent their separate ways. My mother Dorothy took her grumblings, her rancorousness and her suspicions off with her to a new life in Totley, where she lived for another nigh on thirty years, neither more nor less happy than she had been in Fir Vale. Well, perhaps a bit less happy at times because she didn't know enough people to complain about.

Is it by any chance likely that *I* was the one who photographed this scene, using my mother's old Brownie Bakelite camera? The one that we always kept in its brown cloth case (with neat brown plastic piping round the edges), all buttoned down with a press stud for safe keeping, in a very particular drawer in the tallboy that lived in Nanny and Papa's front bedroom overlooking the street? That bedroom would be the one just above the car with the L plate attached with wire to its front bumper. You can see for yourself how neatly it's tucked in beside the causey, directly outside our front door, which would have been flushed with plywood by my grandfather Harold by then, and painted maroon to look as modern as 1965 felt.

Sadly, I didn't take it – as that would have made tracing the copyright holder easier than it proved to be. It was in fact taken by Harry Ainscough (www.copperbeechstudios.co.uk)

I would have been sixteen when this picture of Coningsby Road was taken. Actually, you can nearly see two streets here, one at right angles to the other, fitted in to each other just like a T-square, if you look carefully. See that gas lamp on the left? That's where the top of Blyde Road began, which ran down to Fir Vale Bottom and the shops. That green, cast-iron gas lamp with the flaky paint you can just about glimpse on the street corner was always very good for gripping on to, one arm outstretched, and racing round and round and round in a circle, going faster and faster and faster, until, when you let go, you felt as giddy and staggery giggly-happy as any drunk that ever rolled out of the Cannon Hall on a Saturday night on the arm of his missus, herself a bit tiddly on titchy bottles of Babycham, the drink for ladies who had to keep one eye out for respectability.

Pat, Haydn and the barrelly quiff

Is that car really my sister's boyfriend's second-hand Ford Anglia though? I believe it is. You could never keep him away from our house in Fir Vale when they were first courting. *It's him again*, my mother used to say, face set in stone. She never much wanted him in our house. She'd never let them be alone. She'd always stay up till all hours, keeping guard, frowning at the clock on the mantelpiece, feeling disgusted just to think what they might or might not be getting up to, and waiting and waiting for them to come in from all that canoodling in the gennel, all smiles, all shivers, when they did eventually turn up. Then she'd give them that look of hers. It were just like thunder.

I loved seeing him though, Haydn, Pat's lad, the way he stood in front of our kitchen mirror, working away with that black plastic comb of his on his big, barrelly quiff, so black and so glossy, with his knees flexed, leaning back, getting it just right. Then, oh so carefully, position his cap on the back of his head so that it wouldn't get squashed. He were quite a looker was Haydn. Even Dorothy had to admit that, Attercliffe or no Attercliffe, common as muck or not.

Michael with the family Brownie on Holiday in Blackpool, c.1964

It was the only camera that we ever owned, that Brownie, and we used to take it with us on our week's summer holiday by coach to Mrs Ansell's Boarding House in Blackpool in August, regular as clockwork, just in case anybody felt like depressing the black shutter on a proud family group in holiday mood – five of us in all, comprising me, my mother Dorothy, older sister Pat, and nanny and papa (my grandparents) – all kitted out in their best clothes, driving their legs along that blustery, rain-spitting Promenade, eating battered fish and crozzly chips to their hearts' content.

It was a great street for playing out in, Coningsby Road, in those days because there were so few cars. Even in this picture there are only two. Hardly anybody had cars in those days. You could ride your bikes end to end hell for leather, never bothering your head over traffic. The only traffic I remember were the coal lorry, the horse-drawn gypsy carts – you could exchange old clothes for pegs and balloons – and the big men in their leather aprons who used to deliver wooden barrels of beer to the beer-off, rolling them down our gennel, and then suddenly twirling them round on their ends as if they were light as spinning tops, before sending them down the wooden chute into the beer-off's cellar. Loads of people had tellies by then though! Just look at that bristle of aerials beside the chimney tops...

Yes, fifteen years old I would have been – or thereabouts – when I posed with that Brownie. I'd already made the great change from primary to secondary school, which in my case had meant getting used to wearing a maroon blazer and a snug fitting maroon cap, and taking myself off up Barnsley Road, preferably on my newish Sun *Soleil d'Or* bike – what a sweat of a steep hill that was! – to Firth Park Grammar School. That bike had cost ten pounds, which meant several of the best Christmases you'd ever have all rolled up into one. She might have been kidding though. Fingers crossed.

Everything that Happens in Our Back Yard at Coningsby Road

Rent man comes by wi' his pencil and book
From John Smith the Brewers
To note down payments.
Papa 'ands it ovver at t' door.
No smilin'.

Coal man bustles down t' yard
Wi' his face all black,
In his cap, 'eavin a sack,
Flashin' his white teeth at mum.
She smiles back, sharpish.

When gypsy cart stops in t' street
For owd clothes,
We get pegs in exchange.
They're good for ends of noses –
And for peggin' ont' t' washing line
Strung across back yard
Me sister's saggy blue knickers.

The Demolition of 45 Coningsby Road

The long, slow defiance of cold bedrooms.
The perfect plausibility of stairs.
The pent embarrassment of shuttered closets.
The waiting and the waiting of a chair.

The unexpected heartache of small windows.
The pleasurable fever of the leaf.
The nasty little promise of a knife's edge.
The consequence of air, whirled into grief.

The nature, lackadaisical, of scissors.
One hot, remembered corner, all my life…
The coming and the going and the coming.
The filling and the emptying. The blight.

The tearing down of walls. The strokes of hammers.
The fissuring of glass. The shapes of mouths.
A sledge's dirty burial, with ashes.
The gradual retreat. The candle out.

The Gas Lamp at the Top of Blyde Road

When the gas lamp comes on,
we'll be out there again,
making the usual racket –
hoola hoops, tag, hopscotch,
riding our Christmas bikes.
There will be no stopping us,
will there, tonight?

Loving Pen Knives

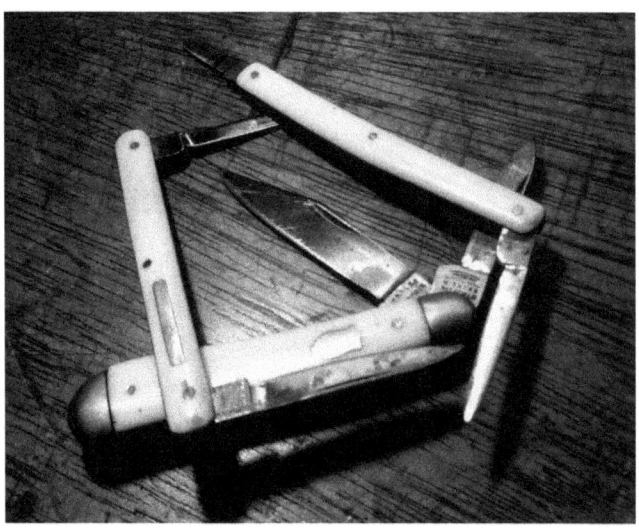

Pen knives were everywhere in Coningsby Road, local-made Sheffield knives, in the wooden cutlery drawer, or on shelves, minding their own business, or deep in men's trouser pockets, mixed in with the coppers. You used to look out for the name of the maker in tiny writing at the flattened end of the blade, just where it met the hinge. Wingfield Rowbotham of Tenter Street. Witners. No man or boy went out without a pen knife in his pocket. Knives were in the blood.

I used to watch my grandfather Harold sharpening the carving knife on a steel, stropping it on one side of the blade and then the other, turning it over quick as a flash, fencing with himself, at Saturday dinner times, with Workers Playtime blaring out on the radio in the kitchen, just before the joint of beef was whipped out of the range, all a pother of steam, with its lovely, black crozzly outside bits, and the gravy got poured in a long, thick, slow stream of brown, into the gravy boat. No knife's worth its salt, he used to say, without a good, keen edge, and you could only test for that by sliding the ball of your thumb down it from top to bottom. That's what he did, sometimes drawing a bit of blood. And that's why he sometimes ate his Saturday dinner laughing, with a hankie knotted round his thumb, besmirched with a bit of blood.

Knives were not about danger or violence or gangs. A pen knife, two-bladed, four-bladed, six-bladed or more – on a Saturday morning, I often used to go and ogle a fat, home-grown, sixteen-bladed knife – a sixteen-blader, I ask you! – in a glass display case in the old markets' building down Fargate – was an object of utility. There were few things handier than a knife when you were in a bit of spot. Some of them had little screwdriver blades for whipping out the tiniest of grub screws from a bedroom door knob. Or it might have a tiny blade with a half moon cut out of it for opening a bottle of stout when you had a raging thirst on. You could scrape the dirt out of your nails with a knife, or peel an orange, or dig baccy out of the bottom of the black, whiffy bowl of a pipe, and even dig a lead air gun pellet out of your palm. I once saw a lad do that in the playground at school. There was always a little ridge up the side of the blade so you could ease it up to attention with your thumb nail. There were nowt handier than a knife, that's what they allus said. An we allus agreed.

I liked pen knives, but I liked bigger knives even more, those with long blades narrowing to a point. They didn't half glint in the light. I never thought of these knives that I collected as weaponry of any kind. I used to keep them in a drawer – sometimes they had snuggly leather sheaths – and take them out to admire them and breathe a bit of foggy breath on them before shining them up a bit more on my pullover sleeve – just as my sister might admire a picture of Rock Hudson sprawled out, all legs and white teeth, on a California beach in his swimming trucks in that week's

Photoplay, or my mother might go all daft and swoony over her heartthrob Robert Mitchum brooding all over her from the corner of a shadowy room, muscles straining out of his suit. I got a bit swoony over knives. The best place to buy them was in swap shops down Attercliffe way, where you could trade in a steam engine with its gleaming copper boiler for a knife. You grew out of steam engines. They were for big kids. You never grew out of a knife. A knife was for life. Never new though. You never bought new. Never knew where to.

Before my grandfather Harold went to war at the Somme, he was training to be a maker of pocket knives, a trainee cutler – that's what the census of 1911 says. He hated it though, all that fiddly indoors work, crammed into a small, sweaty workshop for hours at a time with other grumbly blokes. He wanted to be outside, breathing God's fresh air. He never went back to it after the war. He did something even worse, working on roads up Redmires way, that godforsaken hole. There was nothing else. That was the only work there was for war heroes in those days.

The Boundary Wall of the Fir Vale Infirmary

The boundary wall with what remains of the door to the "tramps' ward"

The long boundary wall of the old Fir Vale Infirmary (it changed its name to the Northern General Hospital a year before I left Sheffield to go to university in the south of England), which stretched right up Herries Road – it went past the end of Coningsby Road – helped to define the mood of my childhood. It was red-brick, soaring and indomitable looking, always too high to see behind. Well, not entirely. I could just catch a glimpse of the roofs of some black Victorian buildings huddled behind that wall, but I never got close to them. Walk down to the bottom of Herries Road, and you could see the entrance to the Infirmary, with its grand double gates and its lodge and its acres and acres of grounds and woods stretching away.

There was even a working farm at the top end, on Longley Lane, with horses that used to lean over the wall, waiting for their noses to be stroked, and for their big sloppy mouths to have handsful of tussocky grass pushed at them. I didn't much like doing that. I thought I might lose a hand an' all. I never did though. They weren't bothered about a hand as long as you kept your arm stretched out ramrod straight in front of you, hand flat as a trembly plate, with the grass in a little bunchy, spriggy heap – like hair on your head when it's been messed about with, annoyingly. Their mouths were allus so soft and wet though. Urgh. You had to wipe all the sloppy gunge off on your trousers.

What exactly happened inside the grounds of that Infirmary? As a child, I never got to see. It was one great big excluding wall of mysterious goings on.

Once upon a time there had been a workhouse somewhere inside those huge, sprawling grounds. That had gone long ago. By the time I was growing up, there was what my mother Dorothy always called The Tramps' Ward, with a slight shudder of apprehension as she said it. Tramps took shelter there at nights – it was a kind of hostel, I suppose – and during the day they were free to roam the streets of Fir Vale. I used to see them out and about. My mother Dorothy would point them out to me when we went shopping, my hand in hers. They were such oddities, those men – I don't remember any womenfolk – and always dressed in scruffy, ill-fitting clothes. One, I remember, wore several hats, all at the same time, like some kind of circus trick. It didn't make a blind bit of difference if it happened to be sunny that day. They were often in a hurry, those men, running or skipping, like big soft kids who had never grown up. They terrified me. They fascinated me. And they were just across the road from our house, walking down the far side of Herries Road. I'd see them when I came running, sweating cobs, out of our gennel, often in twos, though the twos didn't seem to be friends, not especially. They didn't talk to each other. They just got up to their various mad antics. Off they went, down Herries Road, going nowhere in particular, past the bus stop where the working men, always so glum and taciturn, queued for the bus down to the steel works in Brightside in the early morning. Some of those tramps, the ones that fancied a walk, headed off to the library at Firth Park because it was warm in there, and you didn't get rained on, and you could sleep quietly in the reference room to your heart's content.

The Door to the Tramps' Ward

The other day I was standing beside Herries Road once again, at the junction with Coningsby Road, on the very spot where my house had once stood (part of Coningsby Road still survives, but not the side where our house used to stand. There are new houses there now), staring at that same, unchanged stretch of stepped wall, the old boundary wall of the Fir Vale Infirmary just across the road from me, which still runs down Herries Road. It looked much less tall now that I was no longer a child. In fact, it resembled a perfectly harmless stretch of old, red-brick wall bathed in late autumn sunlight. Almost benignly protective. How different the same thing can look on different days or at different times of one's life. It so much depends upon what feelings you bring to it.

As I was standing on that corner where the beer-off used to be, I found myself thinking about those tramps, and how they used to frighten me – in spite of the fact that they were never ever threatening. I'm sure they never even noticed me. After all, I was a small and utterly insignificant child. Only one thing ever happened: I used to stare at them and wonder.

Then I began to puzzle over something else. Where exactly was the door that they would have used to get into the tramps' ward? Was it perhaps the grand main entrance to the old Infirmary that is now the entrance to the Northern General Hospital?

For some reason I found myself thinking – perhaps I was even half-remembering – that there had been a different door. Then I spotted something: not exactly a hole in the wall, but a patch of green, wooden in-filling where there had once been an opening, quite close to the bottom of Herries Road. That was the place then. That's where the door used to be. That's where they used to gather, in a kind of noisy rabble, to go in for the night, and leave again in the mornings to wander the streets.

What I know now – and didn't know then – was that it was hard being a vagrant in Fir Vale in those days. This vagrants' ward – that was its real name; tramps' ward was an invention of my mother's – was not a hostel for the homeless as we know it now. There was a touch of the Victorian attitude towards the undeserving poor still lingering around, in spite of the fact that we were by then living in the 1950s. It involved a certain amount of disapproval and even chastisement. There was lodging of a kind on offer to the needy, but it could never be described as comfortable, and there was no sense that you were being welcomed into a kind of haven of peace and security, albeit temporarily.

On the first night, vagrants had to sleep in one of fifty-seven harsh, dark, confining, cell-like cubicles. They were like small brick boxes. The bed was attached to the wall, and you had to pull it down to lie on it. There was barely room to stand up once the bed was down. Some cells had two doors, one that you came in by, the other that led directly into a work area. The second night was spent in what was generally known as 'The Tramps Palace', which later changed its name to Milton Ward. Once admitted, you were given a bath, a towel and a nightshirt and, if necessary, fumigated. It you had more than two shillings about your person, it might have to be used to pay for your upkeep. No cigarettes or tobacco were allowed. Personal belongings were kept stowed away in a designated pigeon hole. Vagrants sometimes preferred to hide them in a hedge or leave them with a local shopkeeper on the other side of the wall.

Even if you had no money, this help was not exactly free. Sheffield Corporation was not in the business of giving vagrants something for nothing. They had to do one day's work for two nights' shelter, but if one of those days was a Sunday, they could have an extra night. This explains why there was always such a clamour for admittance on a Friday night.

And what sort of work was it that they had to do? Breaking big stones was one option, into small enough pieces to push through a grill. Another regular job was reducing railway sleepers to sticks, first sawing them up into six-inch logs, and then chopping and bundling them for sale to local retailers. Women often picked oakum, helped in the laundry or cleaned. It was no more and no less than *Oliver Twist* transported to the north of England. There was food to be had too – but it was hard, meagre fare. Nor could you linger about the place during the day if you were not working. Vagrants had to leave by seven in the morning, and they were not re-admitted until six o'clock in the evening at the earliest – hence that rabble out on the street in the late afternoon. The door was locked at eleven o'clock. No admissions after that.

Records were kept of the kind of food and drink that vagrants were given. Here is what your daily ration would have been if you had been an occupant of Fir Vale Vagrants' Ward in 1900 (it was the same food for breakfast and supper): 4 oz of bread, 1 oz of margarine and 1 pint of gruel. If there was any gruel left over after everyone had had their allotted pint, it was shared out equally. At dinner time, men were given 8 oz of bread and 2 oz of cheese, and women (evidently less needy) 6 oz of bread and 1.5 oz of cheese. For dinner it was rice, cheese and potatoes. Your last meal before departure might be 8 oz of bread and 2 oz of cheese. By 1930, 2 oz of corned beef were spicing things up a little.

If my mother had known any of this, would she have thought more kindly of these poor creatures sleeping during the day in the Reference Room of Firth Park Library?

The Vagrants' Ward was closed in the 1960s.

New Wood for Old

The entrance to Hinde Common Wood

No matter how dilapidated some of the buildings of north Sheffield may seem to be, nature offers its own glorious compensation for man's neglect, as if in proud defiance of the worst that man can do. I am thinking this to myself as I stand exactly where my demolished home used to be, at the northern end of Coningsby Road, facing the old, stepped, red-brick wall of the Fir Vale Infirmary, which changed its name to the Northern General Hospital in 1967.

Blyde Road, which existed at right angles to Coningsby Road when I was a child, was reduced to rubble long before Coningsby Road was pulverised by the demolition men. A long row of late-nineteenth-century terraced housing, with intermittent gennels that admitted the visitor to asphalted back yards, complete with beaten up dustbins and clusters of back-to-back outside privies, it seemed remarkably similar to

Coningsby Road in appearance. After that street was demolished, the land stood empty for years, gathering rubbish, an unloved no-man's land. Now it boasts a line of mature trees, processing almost all the way down to Fir Vale Bottom. What is more, trees in this part of Sheffield look more healthy and more benign these days. Then, if they existed at all, they would look spiky, black, threateningly twisty and wizened, with patches of black, flaking bark, like old men near doubled over with emphysema. They never gave the impression that they were flourishing; rather, that they were fighting for their lives.

I am reminded once more of this taming and relaxing of nature, almost a quiet air of celebration, half an hour later when I walk up Firth Park Road, past Page Hall, in the general direction of Firth Park and the old Firth Park Library.

Just before you reached that library, on the right hand side of the road, there had always been a stretch of untamed woodland, rising up steeply from the road, that was always closed off to the visitor by a length of tall, green, cast-iron fencing. I always felt fearful of that place as a child. You could see, as you stared through the railings, that the land fell away into a narrow ravine of sorts, before it quickly rose uphill again. I mistrusted the spot for various reasons. I could never quite see where it ended. The ravine looked greasy and sticky-wet with pollution and old rubbish. And we were not allowed into it. It was entirely closed off to us. Perhaps it was too dangerous to enter for one reason or another.

Today, just as I reach the corner of the old Firth Park Library building, I see that something interesting has happened. That forbidding sliver of woodland has now been given a name, an identity. What is more, there is a sign, with an entrance, an invitation to take a path through this very patch of nameless wood that as a child I had never been allowed to enter. Having first examined the sign, and noted the name – Hinde Common Wood – I pass through, and start to walk a meandering path up this beckoning swell of a rising hillside, which climbs gradually towards Hinde House Lane, where I exit again. My only sadness is that it is so rubbish-strewn – crisp packets, plastic bottles, streamers of white lavatory paper, lager cans, polystyrene take-away cartons...

The Death of The Sunbeam Cinema, Fir Vale, Sheffield 5

Something terrible happens when you demolish a building. As the wrecker's ball swings at the surprisingly fragile facade – how easily it goes down! – everything that ever once happened there seems to disperse in a welter of filthy, unlovely, throat-catching dust. There's a slight feeling of shame and betrayal in the air. Nothing's quite right any more. All those casual-to-urgent conversations, all that laughter and frustration, all those furtive mini-moments of heart-pulsing hand-squeezing in the back corridor, all the relentless humdrumness of the mind-numbing routines of people's lives...Everything goes, between the space of one breath and the next. Or at least that's how it sometimes seems.

And yet there are buildings and buildings. We let go of some buildings more readily than others. Some buildings seem to condemn themselves to drabness and sterility – many banks, for example. Others are like beacons in the night. We live our lives by them. They are our lode stars. They shine out in the darkness. Yes, there are few things more precious and magical than a local cinema.

Below is a poem I wrote about the demolition of the Sunbeam cinema at Fir Vale. I was little more than a child when I saw the building being demolished, and this poem was written many years after that beloved cinema had been reduced to rubble. It is a rather childish poem, written in a deliberately clumsy way, as if to suggest that a child is writing it, as best he can, just pouring out the facts and the feelings. He ends it rather abruptly because it is too upsetting to do anything else. The only thing he can do is to let himself be helplessly dragged away by his mother, as quickly as possible, with a sharp tug of the motherly hand, for a bit of distraction, in order to soothe away all the hurt of his unfathomable loss.

> Nothing's so sad as buildings you once loved
> Being brought down by a ball on a long chain.
> That's how it was with our old cinema,
> The only Sunbeam brightening up Fir Vale.
>
> A wonky line of ragged, laughing kids,
> We'd queue on Sat'day mornings in the rain,
> Waiting for Captain Marvel and his cloak,
> Clutching a bag of sweets and some small change.
>
> It fell in a great pother of brick dust,
> With that ball thumping at the topmost walls.
> I'd hated seeing it boarded up and dead.
> My mum whisked me off shopping to Page Hall.

One afternoon I saw Cliff Richard in *The Young Ones* at the Coliseum on Spital Hill. That was a place I hardly ever went to. It were too far away really, almost in town. It allus felt a bit sad going there, not much like a treat at all. Hardly anybody ever went to it. It felt as if it were dying. Loads of cinemas were dying in them days. You used to see 'em, all boarded up, wi' scrappy, soggy bits of posters hanging off of 'em, flapping in the wind, shouting out about all those films you'd never get to see, not now. The last films they ever showed at the Coliseum were a double bill of *The Horse Without a Head* and *Savage Sam*. That were in November 1963, same month I saw the Beatles at the City Hall for the very last time – third time that year though! The cinemas were dying off. The Beatles were just starting up. That's how it was. You just had to lump it.

It must have been a matinee because I remember it were sunny when we went in, and still light when we came out and did a bit of jigging about beside the bus stop. I don't remember liking Cliff much. He looked a bit like a doll. My sister Pat was a big Elvis fan, and she used to play her Elvis LPs on her Dansette record player, *Jailhouse Rock* and such like. They didn't half boom out. Cliff looked as if he were trying to be Elvis, but not quite managing it. Same hair. Sort of. Same long jacket. Same flashy smile. He danced on a train in that film without once falling off. It were all a bit stupid if you ask me.

Historical Fragments

Those cobbles keep re-emerging on Coningsby Rd

There is everything that we see, know, smell, taste and touch, the palpable reality of our day-to-day lives, and then there is something else that we choose to call history. History is everything that we do not ourselves live through. It begins before we were born, and it stretches back and back. Known through photographs, descriptions, films and books, history has quite a different kind of emotional claim upon us. We do not feel it directly upon our pulses. We always know it indirectly. It is another country altogether. Many millions of dead people live there.

45 Coningsby Road had been lived in by my great-grandmother Emily Nield, my own mother's mother, since at least as early 1911, almost forty years before I was born. Towards the end of my own mother Dorothy's life – she lived in her house in Totley until just a few weeks before her death at the age of 93 in 2009 – I talked to her about the fact that Emily used to do other people's washing to make ends meet, making a fire underneath the copper until it got hot enough to put in the wash, rubbing each flannelette sheet on the

washboard until her knuckles burned, putting it through the mangle, hanging it out all over the kitchen to dry – or out in the backyard if it wasn't raining, or soot wasn't falling from the air. It was all so labour-intensive in those days.

Why was she taking in washing though? Because Emily Nield was a desperate woman by the time she reached middle age at the end of the 1920s. Her husband had been a general dogsbody for the *Sheffield Independent*, moving goods around the city in a horse and cart. One day the horse backed the cart into a narrow passage in the high street, and he fell down a lift shaft, sustaining life-threatening injuries. He died soon after. There was no pension for his widow. She was left alone in Coningsby Road, having to find the weekly rent of four shillings a week from the rent collector who called, regular as clockwork, on behalf of John Smith the Brewers. The government gave her a small weekly payment of five shillings, but it was far too little for survival. So she took in other people's washing in order to make a bit extra.

In the beer-off at top of the yard lived Mrs Proctor, the wife of the publican. She disliked Emily. In fact, she wanted the house to be lived in by someone else. The rules stated that if you received financial support from the government, you were not allowed to make any additional money. Mrs Proctor told the government about Emily and her washing, and the money was stopped.

'She was a real bad 'un, ever so evil, Mrs Proctor,' my mother Dorothy told me at her home in Totley seventy-five years later. 'She had a son called Ben Proctor. He used to tantalise grandma, call her names, set the kids on her.'

After Harold was demobbed from the Sheffield Battalion in 1918, he returned to Fir Vale and the prospect of months or perhaps even years – who was to say? – of poverty-stricken worklessness. Eventually he found a job as a groundsman with the YMCA, looking after their sports fields at Crimicar Lane on the very edge of the city.

Emily Nield, my maternal grandmother, died of pneumonia in 1935, during a visit to Crimicar Lane. That was fourteen years before my birth.

Soon after, my family – Harold, Mabel, Dorothy, Ken and his older brother Norman – moved in to that house in Coningsby Road where she had lived, and I was later to be born. On the day of Emily's funeral, Mrs Proctor took it upon herself to organise a visit to the house by a prospective new tenant from Shire Green, but the woman turned it down. According to my mother, the woman apologised for having intruded upon a funeral, and Mrs Proctor was suitably shamed. The rent had gone up by then – to eight shillings a week.

My mother Dorothy was delighted to move back to the city, with its prospect of shops and a local cinema. Her two brothers felt quite otherwise. They pined for the kind of outdoors life they had enjoyed at Crimicar Lane. Feelings were similarly divided about Emily, their grandmother. When she died unexpectedly, Dorothy was inconsolable. A light in her teenage life had been switched off. A few weeks later I asked Dorothy's brother, my late Uncle Ken, how he had found Emily. He had known her as a tiny boy, the youngest of the family.

'She was horrible to me,' he said. 'When I used to try to hold her round the knees as any small child might, she used to push me away. I couldn't understand why she was treating me like that. I think she resented the fact that as the youngest I was a burden upon Mabel her daughter. Perhaps she was being over-protective. What was she like? She was a conventional poor grandma who wore a bonnet and lace up boots – there was no such thing as fashion in those days. She had a terrible life. No income at all.'

The Second World War ended four years before I was born. And yet the war, because I did not live through it, seems utterly remote to me, almost a thing of myth, full of exaggerated tragedy and heroic extremes. Seldom, as it generally must have been, humdrum and boringly day-to-day. Sheffield was hit by German incendiary bombs, pulverised on two successive nights. Great fires lit up the city centre. My mother, sister, grandmother and grandfather would hurry across the back yard to the Andersen shelter when the sirens sounded. That Andersen shelter, which had already disappeared by the time that I was born, was not a happy place to be. The Germans were not directly to blame for this unhappy state of affairs. Blame instead our next door neighbours, Mrs Moorhouse and her daughter Marjorie, a couple of tall, big-boned women with mouths on who lived together in a perpetual state of low-level warfare.

They would arrive at the shelter heaving armsful of belongings. The reason for this was simple: they did not wish to lose their best things should the house go up in flames. Unfortunately, there was not the space in that shelter to accommodate armsful of belongings – frocks, camisoles, best overcoats, jewellery, bedding. Rows would flare up. Who was responsible for bringing in all this bloody stuff? my furious grandfather would ask them. There's isn't bloody room to breathe in here. Each would accuse the other. The fights between these two women were the stuff of legend. They would howl and scream. They would throw dinner plates at each other. By comparison, the German threat seemed positively mild-mannered that night.

Sid Comes Back from the War, 1945

When he came back on VE Day, I didn't recognise 'im.
Mrs Moorhouse came out from next door, an' she just said:
He's back, Dorothy, Sid's back.
He's left his bags at neighbour's. Gone for a drink.
I fainted when I saw him.

He were completely black from bein' in Burma that long.
He had these long ginger moustaches, waxed at both ends.
No glasses either.
He'd had malaria, diptheria.
He often shook after that.
It were frightenin'.

I didn't want to know him.
He wanted to tek me away wi' 'im, but I didn't want to go.
Then, when I got pregnant wi' you, he said:
Whose do you think *he* is then? He's certainly not mine.
He wouldn't acknowledge you.
He were a reyt bugger, that one.

Firth Park Library

The old Firth Park library

When I was growing up in Fir Vale in the 1950s, our local Firth Park Library was an important looking building created for serious study whose entrance (made all the more pompous by a splendid coat of arms) you approached up a rather reverence-inducing flight of stone steps. It had been built, like the Central Library in town, at the beginning of the 1930s and it was fifteen minutes walk away from our house, if you put your skates on. Don't drop the books from under your arm though. More haste, less speed.

The library had been officially opened by Lord Ponsonby of Shulbrede on 24 July, 1930, and that peer of the realm, who had once been MP for Brightside, was also the first person to sign the visitors' book, with these bland words of official approval: 'This fine library is a credit to the City of Sheffield.' Scanning the visitors' book today – the library finally closed its doors in September 1999 – you would be hard pressed to find a comment written by an ordinary reader from the streets of Sheffield. The most curious entry of all was written in 1965, not long after Dr Beeching had axed a good part of our national rail network. Dated in Latin numerals – X VII MXMLXV – a woman called Ms Anne from Canterbury, who describes herself as a student pilgrim, writes: 'This branch has high potentiality in one of Dr Beeching's redundant waiting rooms.' Is this to be construed as blame or praise? The question hangs in the air.

Generously proportioned and light-filled, Firth Park Library had a separate reference room with heavy, hard-to-shift chairs and tables at which you could pursue your individual studies. Open newspapers were on display on sloping wooden stands – from the *Liverpool Daily Post* to the *Daily Mail*. Men were forever standing reading at those stands in their scruffy brown rain coats. In those years, regional newspapers had very distinctive voices. Lots of people worked for them. There were special correspondents for this, that and the other. One of them even came to our house once, though I don't remember why. Just that he did, and that everybody got excited. We always took the *Sheffield Star* and the *Sheffield Telegraph* at home, and my grandfather Harold would spend hours sitting behind his paper, lost to view – they were big things, not finicky little tabloid affairs as they tend to be these days – behind one or another of those open papers in his favourite chair. My favourite bit of the paper, being a little kiddo and too silly to know any better, was Gloops the cartoon in the *Star*. I never stopped laughing.

The whole family borrowed books from Firth Park Library – my mother Dorothy's favourites were historical romances by the likes of Jean Plaidy and Georgette Heyer. (She read her books after everyone had gone to bed, during her smoking hour. *Players Please* – that's what the ad said – or Woodbines in those tiny, thin, green packs of five, since you're asking). Tramps, perfectly harmless, were often to be found sleeping at the tables in the reading room. There was also a separate room, more like its own little library, for children's books, where I used to go to borrow my un-put-downable *Famous Five* or *Secret Seven* books by Enid Blyton. Or perhaps *Just William* or *Jennings*...

Using your library tickets, and having your books stamped out when you handed them over, were solemn and important rituals – I remember that you had to hand over your books to the librarian, together with your library tickets, which were kept safe in a little cardboard wallet. You were allowed to take out a maximum of six books at a time, and the space through which you had to pass in order to do so felt quite narrow, which made the whole process a bit worrying. It was a little like passing through airport security in our day. The librarian's desk was high, and the librarian, gripping her rubber stamp held high in the air, was frowning down at you. So as a child you always found yourself handing them up – rather than across. Of course, if the books were late back – the date of return was stamped onto a sheet of paper that was glued into the front of the book itself – you had to pay a fine... Everybody got cross about that.

I remember so well staring at particular books in the sometimes difficult-to-reach stacks, and deciding that at a certain point I would need to read them if I were ever to regard myself as well educated – several volumes of the collected works of the great nineteenth century Russian novelist Dostoyevsky, translated by Constance Garnett, for example, in their distinctive red and yellow covers. I also remember, as a sixth former at Firth Park Grammar School, telling myself that if I were ever really to get to grips with world affairs, I would have to master economics, and there was a particularly large guide to world economics in the library at which I used to stare up, aspirationally. Did I ever actually borrow it? Perhaps not. I certainly do not remember ever profiting by it.

The other wonder of the library was that it was just a short distance away from the Boating Pond where we used to sail our model yachts when there was enough of a breeze to do so. My mother bought me a yacht from Blackpool one year with that very pond in mind. The pond disappeared long ago. The space was later used for a concrete basketball court which looked abandoned and woebegone when I last saw it. Now it's been cleaned up and made to look much more cheerful and people-welcoming again.

Firth Park Library had one other precious quality. That was the nature of its silence. That library was not as many libraries are these days. It was not a place of conversation. It was not to be mistaken for the butcher's shop or a street corner where people gassed to their heart's content. It was a building set apart for reading and for choosing the books you might want to read, and to do that you needed silence. You cannot both read and do other things. Education was a precious thing. With education you could change your life. You were no longer at the mercy of the decision-making powers of other people. The rule was strictly enforced in the Reference Room, but even in the library proper you seldom heard a human voice. At worst, there would be a whisper. Everyone respected that rule. Even the tramps never seemed to snore.

Art and the Graves

There was no art at home in the terraced house in Fir Vale, north-east Sheffield where I spent the first nineteen years of my life, no art on the walls, no art books barring one (which was kept in a damp, musty cupboard in the always miserably cold front room), and certainly no conversation about art matters. Art did *not* matter. In fact, it did not really exist at all. Such art as existed outside the home – at Firth Park Grammar School, for example, to which I bicycled, uphill, breaking sweat, every live-long week day for seven long years – was never taken very seriously. Who ever made a living from art? At best, it was a pastime amongst many others. I have one strong memory of an art lesson at school, and it consisted of a discussion about the merits of the lyrics and the music of John Lennon's 'I Am the Walrus'. The year was 1967, and I was eighteen years old.

It was an informal session. I knew that because the art teacher was sitting with his legs drawn up on one of our school desks. He was also in a state of high excitement about what we would now call popular culture, and what in those days was simply called pop music. John Lennon had just rewritten the story of popular music, he said, eyes blazing. I think we were inclined to agree with him. But why were we talking about Lennon anyway on that afternoon? Because he had been to art college in Liverpool? There was no discussion of his art, as far as I can recall. Nor was there any talk of how we might somehow extrapolate from or profit by, creatively, Lennon's example; no references, as there might easily have been, to Surrealism, Dada or even Lewis Carroll.

As for doing art as a subject at school, it was never encouraged. It was an unserious subject. The serious subjects were the academic ones. Art schools were for the idlers, the jokers, the failures, those who were not inclined to take their own futures seriously. I drew caricatures in my spare time, but that was all. My mother, on the other hand, had loved art at school, and she had been a talented drawer, but such talent as she was once said to have possessed must have withered on the vine because during the years of my growing, I cannot recall her ever taking up a pencil or a brush. All I remember having seen were some meticulous pencils drawings of running horses, several on a single page. She never talked about that dead passion, except, on occasions, to make a fleeting reference to it. In fact, the little knowledge about art I began to pick up was acquired indirectly, thanks to studying French literature.

It was entirely accidental, an offshoot of something else. I was studying French literature in the sixth form – Balzac, Baudelaire, Molière, Corneille, Maupassant and others. Our teacher urged us to look more widely, to try to put what we were studying into some broader context. So my mother bought me three anthologies of French prose and poetry by Lagarde & Michard from Wards Bookshop down Chapel Walk, covering the seventeenth, nineteenth and twentieth centuries. Goodness knows why the eighteenth century was so conspicuously absent. I was enthralled by these handsome hardback books with their blue covers. But it was not the extracts from novels, poems and plays alone that pleased me. Each one came illustrated with colour plates of the art of the period. There, for example, in the volume devoted to the twentieth century, were colour plates of reproductions of paintings by Georges Rouault, Yves Tanguy, Georges Braque and others.

I had never seen such enthrallingly skewed versions of reality. When my eyes encountered these paintings, I felt as if I were a diver descending into a pool of an incalculable depth. I had never seen colour used in such ways. I had never seen the human form distorted in quite the way that some of these French artists distorted it. It was like nothing that I had ever seen with my eyes, but some part of me knew that, in essence, it seemed – and, more important, felt, on my pulses – to be even realer than the real. How could that possibly be true though? Some quest had begun.

There was an art gallery in Sheffield too that I began to visit as a teenager. It was called the Graves, and it lived on an upper floor of the Central Library in the middle of town. I would go to that library to read and to study, and after I had done my allotted portion of studying – which included, I remember, readings the Songs and Sonnets of John Donne at a table in the Reference Library – I would mount the rather serious looking, angular, '30s staircase to the Graves Art Gallery upstairs. Before entering, I would look at the portrait of its founder, Dr Graves himself, whose image always kept an eye on visitors, as if to judge their suitability. He was not in fact a medical doctor, though I always thought that he looked rather like one. There was something pleasingly, dependably, reassuringly avuncular about that portrait.

The Graves is little changed in nearly three-quarters of a century. It was always a quiet, sequestered plot. It always felt as if it was waiting to be discovered by the likes of...well, me. And there on the walls were a handful of paintings that I got to know rather well, including a flecky, impressionistic, early twentieth-century seaside view called 'Beach at Ambleteuse' by the famously dissipated English artist Charles Conder. There were such overdressed belles on French beaches in those days! Yes, what fascinated me in part about this painting was how fashionable a place this seemed to be, so different from the beaches of Skegness, Blackpool, Filey or Cleethorpes. It was a beach where the prosperous bourgeoisie went to see and be seen – and perhaps little more than that. There was no hint of any frolicking about in the sea, no stripping down to very little at all – the bit I always liked about a beach – merely idle posturing and lounging about in extraordinarily elaborate clothing. And where were the children? Weren't beaches about children having a good time? Art could – and did – transport you to such strange places.

In the Kitchen at 45 Coningsby Road: a Homage to the Wireless

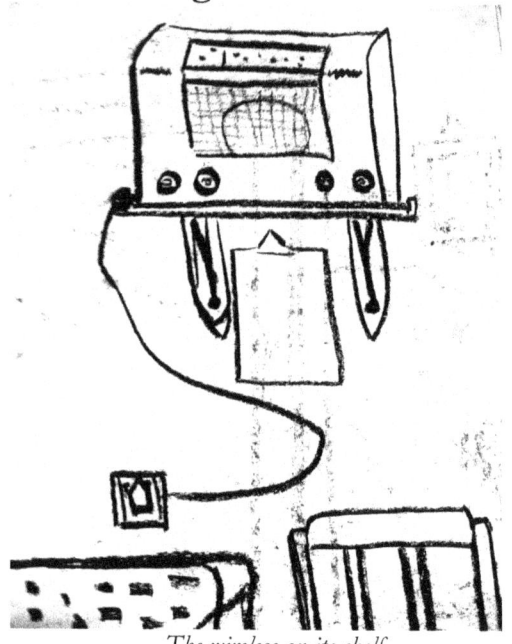

The wireless on its shelf

Every room has a place where the eye naturally comes to rest. Sometimes we glance fondly in the direction of a favourite chair, anticipating minutes, hours, days of blessed future ease. In the draughty medieval hall, the focus of attention would have been the great fireplace, where humans would gather to unthaw their near-frozen limbs in winter, and whisperingly plot future vengeance upon their near-frozen relatives just over the hill. In India, the focus of attention is more likely to be the family shrine, with its gentle, sweet-smelling clutter of fading flower garlands, family portraits, and statues of favourite dancing gods miraculously equipped with a multiplicity of arms.

In our small kitchen at Coningsby Road, we were blessed with two such places – an open range, where, thanks to my grandfather Harold's careful minding, coal blazed from dawn until ten at night, and, high on a wall nearby, a brown bakelite wireless, large, heavy, blockish, commanding, which was also entirely within the control of my grandfather. It was he who provided heat. It was also he who guarded the portals of knowledge.

He was the one who would reach up to switch it on at the appointed hour. It was he who was in control of the programmes to which we would dutifully listen. The key moments in the day were noon and six o'clock in the evening, when the news bulletins would ring out, solemnly. They were not to be missed. It is unimaginable that we would listen to anything else at those hours. Or do anything else. Nothing else would be adequate to those minutes. At such times as these, the world rushed in, often alarmingly, to disturb our localness. When the Soviet tanks rolled into Prague in 1968, displacing Alexander Dubcek, we listened to heady reports of the brutal Soviet incursion into its satellite state on our wireless at Coningsby Road. We knew that Dubcek had been snuffed out as a significant player in the game of global politics. At other times, Harold was happy for us to be light-entertained to our hearts' content. At Saturday dinner time, as the week's bottles of Tizer and Lemonade were being dutifully lifted onto the dinner table, and Harold was standing beside the joint of beef, briskly sharpening up the carving knife with a steel, Workers Playtime would start up on the wireless, presented by cheery Sam Costa, to the timeless accompaniment of rousingly optimistic music.

I often stared in near awe up at that wireless, thinking about what it gave us. I would marvel at the disc in the centre, which would light up when it was switched on, and at the needle which would swing from left to right through the world's stations as my grandfather twisted the tuner, enabling us to listen to a great bibbly-babble of mingled foreign tongues and tunes, winging in from everywhere, and all passing through and past at lightning speed.

Why up so high though? The wireless needed to be far beyond the reach of the fingers of meddlesome children – and quite deliberately so. I have mentioned elsewhere in this book that there was no art at Coningsby Road. That is not quite true. As a child, I indulged in art of a rough-and-ready, untutored kind, and even my mother, when the mood seized her, would make a drawing of a favourite horse she had once known at Crimicar Lane. She never, to my knowledge, ever finished any of her drawings. They were always fragmentary, abandoned. Mine I usually finished. The reason for this is simple. I was fast and slap-dash in my habits. The job was over and done in no time at all. I didn't have the patience – nor the necessary skills – to profit by slowness.

At the start of this chapter there is a charcoal drawing I made one day in my Rowney Sketch Pad of that wireless, raised up high on its sacred perch. I was thirteen years old at the time, in Form 3A at the Grammar School as I have noted on one of its pages. There it is, high on the wall, almost grazing our kitchen ceiling, supported by a pair of stout metal brackets screwed into the wall. Harold painted and put up those brackets, and the little wooden shelf on which the wireless sits too, so high in the air out of harm's way. The glowing disc that used to light up as soon as the radio was switched on – it took a little while before you heard any sound – is hidden behind gauze meshing which I have indicated by some criss-cross marks. Beneath the wireless is our calendar, telling us about the obligations of the days and the weeks, and beneath that, an upright chair to sit on and a pullover letting itself hang dry over another chair back, having edged up fairly close to the open fire.

The open fire

And what of the open fire? That too was a place of marvels, and it too found a place in that sketch book, memorialised as a sacred nook. An open fire is a place for dreaming. There are few things quite so changeable as the shapes made by fragmenting and collapsing bits of coal. Flames, too, are marvels of unpredictability, flaring up like great orchestras one moment, and then dying away to the saddest and tiniest of sputtery peeps. I would squat in front of that fire making toast on the old iron toasting fork – which was, as its name suggests, a long, two-pronged fork off which, from time to time, the thin slices of white toast, bending and browning so beautifully one minute, would suddenly pitch forward into the flames. Or I might get distracted by a passing thought and notice, by a shout from my mother – who was probably clearing the table at my back – that black smoke was pothering up from the end of the fork, and all that was left of my toast was a brittle rectangle of unchewable and wholly inedible hardness.

Sometimes my mother Dorothy would snatch the slice of toast off the end of the toasting fork and, having jumped it around in her hands a bit, scratch off all the black dusty stuff with a knife blade. I could eat it at the table then, all beautifully scraped back to the usual golden toasty colour.

After that, she used to flap all that black dust off her apron and back into the fire.

Early Morning, 45 Coningsby Road, Sheffield, 1956

Someone is waiting to ignite the fire.
The fuel's all there – coal, faggots, paper spills.
Someone's stooped over, coughing, by the range,
An old man, with black fingers, peering up

Into the dark interior above,
Its soot-caked sides... Is something really there?
He's heard a scuffle. Summat's not quite reyt...
Up goes that hand, a third time, reaching round...

All of a rush, it comes, pink, blotchy-black.
He cups it in his palm. It's warm as toast.
Mabs! he shouts up. There's scuffling upstairs.
All of a rush she comes, and takes the bird.

In the Kitchen at 45 Coningsby Road in 1957

On t' floor by t' roll-top secretaire,
There were an owd blue flock rug.

Bits used to come off it when you pulled.
Lift up corner (if you dared),
An' you'd get slimy silver fish dartin' everywhere.

Toastin' fork stood on its prongy legs in t' grate.
Stick toast on t' prong ends…
Next thing, toast's black as death wi' chokin' smoke.
Fire spat out bits o' coyl an' all.
Nanny said you 'ad to watch it.

Bath neet were great, every Thursday.
Zinc bath heaved up from t' cellar.
Blankets coverin' t' clothes 'orse
In front o' t' fire
To mek it private.

When t' kettle whistled,
There were a deafenin' racket.
Umpteen pans an' buckets
O' pourin', boilin' watter.
Stick a toe in too smartish,
You'd whip it straight out again, bawlin'.

Sittin' in t' bath, starin' at fire,
Nowt but yoursen,
Behind that clothes horse,
Just wallowin', in a dream, legs thrashin',
In a big tub o' steamin' watter…

After you came yer sister.
Same watter,
Wi' a bit more added.
Bein' 'er, there were scent an' pongy stuff after.

In a Bit of a Spin about Old Money

There was much rattling of coins in pockets, male trouser pockets, at Coningsby Road, and often in front of the open fire so that you could warm your backside, and flex your knees a bit, and gently rock back and forth, and smile back at whichever little 'un was looking and cheeky-chappying back up at you, as you thought about prosperity, and all that it meant at six-o'clockin-off hour on a Friday night, with the whole weekend stretchin' ahead to play with and play for, long as the Vegas Strip.

It was what they did back then, men with the luck to have paid jobs, but I remember my uncle and my grandfather at it especially, running their fingers through their coins, letting them jangle and chink and slip around in their trouser pockets, while the womenfolk tutted as they clatter-banged with the dishes at the sink because that pocket'd be in holes and good for nothing at all before the night was out at that rate. That didn't stop them though, because it made them feel well off, didn't it, it made them feel they were somebody, letting all those coins slip through their fingers, it made them feel they were worth a bob or two.

There were so many of them an' all, and all in different shapes and sizes and colours and metals – titchy farthings, ha'pennies, big coppers sometimes so smooth and thin and old, with Britannia with her shield and her trident on one side, and Queen Victoria in her pony tail. Then there were threepenny bits, silver sixpences, shillings, florins, half crowns.... Where would it ever end? It made you absolutely brilliant at mental arithmetic when there were 240 pence to the pound, when your mother told you to keep on top of whatever it was you'd bought at the butcher's shop and the fishmonger and Banners the haberdashery on Fir Vale Bottom, and Socketts for all your electricals. Coins were good for playing with an' all, shove halfpenny, or twirling them in your fingers to see whose could stay up longest, watchin' it wobblin' and lurching like a drunk before it fell over.

Don't lose them though. Don't let them run away with you down the drain in the back yard or there'd be a right set to then. Money were money after all.

Lovely Things in Fir Vale, 1964

Chopped pork from the beer-off.
Lemon and Lime from Latham's.
Burns a hole in your pocket on Sat'day, does
Friday night's savings.

Sheffield Tobacco Smoke

Bitter and acrid,
It'd catch at the back of your throat,

all that manly puffed out tobacco smoke,
when you sat on the tram's top deck, lookin' down,
proud to be nearly drivin',
with coins janglin' in your pocket
and the whole of Sat'day morning in town –
from Lady's Bridge, on up through Haymarket to Fargate –
spread out before you
like a fat slice of Wilf's chewy parkin.

Drunken Domesticity: Sheffield, 1954

One man shouts in a room, to huge effect.
A small child cringes – down to finger height.
A woman flings an arm out, desperate.
The man withdraws. His boots ring down the night.

A child's tear glistens on a red, pulped cheek.
The woman chinks a cup, so delicate.
Loud, bitter breath is fogging up the streets.
The child is in his bed, and doesn't sleep.

The man stabs at the lock with hazy aim.
He swears, then hammers. Swears. It opens up.
Pale light falls on the lino's greasy grain,
And on that doormat too, which reads GOOD LUCK.

Playtime At Firs Hill School

When you got let out for mornin' playtime, after you'd drunk your milk from t' crate, and wiped creamy bit on t' rim at top off o' your face, an' licked extra bit of cream off crinkly silver cap an' all, you used to run from end to end o' t' playground just for the sake of it, shoutin' an wavin' your arms about. When you went a cropper, it were hard on your knees. Nubdy picked you up. It were girly to expect it. You picked yersen up. Football were best, just beltin' that ball. Not scoring, just beltin' it. Michael Parkin were blindin' at dribblin', wi' 'is socks rolled down to his ankles. An' 'is trouser tops rolled up an' all. I don't remember owt else but dashin' abaht an' screamin', so there's nowt else to be said. That's just what we did at Firs Hill at playtime, I'm not kiddin' on either.

One Hundred Lines

Summat takes me back to that yard
Where I see little kids through a winder
jostlin' wi' a ball, and Bill,
Who's starin' in at me, mouthin'
Where've you tekken your 'ook to, then?
I'm doin' them lines, my look says.
He nods, runs off.

I must not kick a ball at window panes.
I write it once, and then again, again.
My hand's all numb. Outside they're goin' mad,
Beltin' that ball across the yard and back.
Parkie's playin' a blinder, weavin' in an out,
Shorts rolled way up, grey socks way down…

It weren't my fault though,
I'm thinkin', frownin' to mesen,
Parkie just lobbed it reyt onto my foot.
It just sprung up from me toe end.
Weren't nowt I could do but look.
Honest, sir.

Ball just bounced up.
Next thing: smash.
An' that were that.

Three Cheers for Gas at Coningsby Road!

Chips in that frying pan crozzling away are the fiercest things you'll see today, spitting and crackling above the telly, gobbing great balls of fat, making t' bedrooms smelly… It's great, this cooker though – and not just for chips! It boils up water, fries mum's fish, makes kettles whistle and tremble and spurt. You can't see our kitchen for all the murk. And inside, while all that's going on, there's a big, juicy joint of best spring lamb coming along…

It's gas, you know – it's fast, is gas! Bit frightening though, way it flares up when you just touch it wi' a match. And when you blow, it leans and shudders – or goes right out if you flap this cupboard. That's bad though. Mum gets mad at that. She says it's dangerous to mess with gas. She's reyt an' all. One kid in our class lost half his hair muckin' about like that…

Back Yard Scene, 45 Coningsby Road, Fir Vale, Sheffield 1958

My mother ran and whisked the washing in.
The soot flakes fell, black snow from a grey sky.
The beer barrels came trundling along,
With surly men in aprons by their side.

The shelter that had kept the Germans out
Stood staunch and ugly by the lavvy doors.
We crept in there to hear our voices shout
Out swear words, tell real ghost stories, lose balls.

An outside lavvy's not a bad thing though,
Especially when the greens make you feel sick.
I stuffed them in my cheeks like hamsters do,
And shot them out in bits. The water flicked.

Double Sheffield Portrait

She owned him lock, stock and barrel.
She owned the trousers that depended from his shanks.
She owned the gloves that muffled his creaky fingers.
She owned every last part of him, with small thanks.

She owned him lock, stock and barrel.
She owned his whistle, reedy, across the pond.
She owned the saliva in his mouth, and the roaring
  in his chest.
She owned the busyness of his words,
  and his small and finicky infuriations.
She owned the pots and pans that hung amidst
  the tools in his dank and lonely shed.
She owned his life, such as it was.

He owned her, lock, stock and barrel.
He owned how she glared at him long and long,
  like motor car headlights left on in the night.
He owned the gristle in her voice, and the stamp
  of her ungainly hoof.
He owned her buttocks, her ears, those tufty sprigs
  that showered out from each ear.
He owned every last part of her, and he made of her
  what he could.

Saturday, Sheffield, 11.55pm

Likely as not I'll make it to the street,
Then vomit on the pavement, sour and sweet,
The lot of it, quick-shovelled in, now out,
With all that ale, Niagara-belched, in one great gout.

Now I feel better, champion you might say,
My eye as level as this wall you'll see
Beyond the window, as I storm through the door,
Bent over, ready for man's task once more.

The Star Walk

The Star Walk 1966 – picture courtesy of The Sheffield Star

Crowds of people, all neighbours of ours from along the street, used to go streaming down Blyde Road to Fir Vale Bottom, pushing and shoving, to get to just near the tram stop up to Lane Top, to watch the walkers in their white vests streaming or straggling past, thousands of them, cheering on their favourites. There weren't any trams just then though, not on that morning. If you wanted to get somewhere that morning, it had to be shank's pony. They stopped the trams to let the walkers take up the road space.

Oh aye, it were a big thing in those days, the Star Walk. Every year it went off, on the Tuesday straight after Whitsunday. Thousands entered. You got a pie and a pint if you won, and a bit of paper sayin' you'd won, well done lad. Only amateurs or novices were allowed to enter, and you had to live within a thirty miles radius of Sheffield Town Hall. We used to mark it in biro on the calendar in the kitchen with a big red ring. They used to train for months, them walkers. It were a rum affair though, that's what my mother Dorothy used to say. I loved it though. I loved watching the way they walked, most of them youngish blokes in long baggy shorts with numbers tied to their fronts. Was it really a run more than a walk though? If it were, it were never reyt fast, not like a real run. Not like a hundred-yard sprint at school, say. Not quite. Not really.

It were a sort of half-running waddle, a heel-to-toe affair. Blokes used to twist their shoulders this way and that as if they'd yank their arms out of their sockets, and walk, with a sort of rum hip-rolling gait, on the sides of their feet, in their black boots, with the socks rolled down to their ankles, as if they'd got bunions like nanny had or such like. No trainers in them days. Nothing to make it easier.

Why couldn't they run like real runners? I used to ask myself as a little kid. I could never quite fathom it. Then I suddenly got it. They were walkin' like that because you weren't allowed to run. It were a walk, weren't it, you daft devil? They were walking like that, twisting to the side and waddlin', with their elbows pumpin' out like billyo, to make themselves go as fast as they could without actually running. That were the whole point of it. It didn't half make you laugh to see how some of 'em did it. They made a right old spectacle of themselves. Straight out of that Ministry of Silly Walks if you ask me. It were great though, I know that. Thousands watched and cheered. It were a reyt heaving crush when first ones went by. Cheering were deafening. You had to block your ears – if you could move your arms at all.

Owlerton were where it finished. What a flippin' slog, they allus said, blokes that did it. Made you thirsty all right.

Casually Damned: the unanswerable verdict of the School Report

Report-fearful: sultry schoolboy at Firth Park Grammar School anticipates the worst in 1962

School reports. The good, the bad, the indifferent. The sight of them, unmistakable, on the bristly brown door mat, in their sleek white envelopes blue-stamped CONFIDENTIAL, thrust through the letter box and fallen down there, so carelessly askew, as if belying their importance in any young life.

The words you try not to flinch from when your mother, having opened the envelope boldly addressed to her alone, and unfolded the single long sheet of paper, reads them out to you, subject by subject, ending with Sport, before the summaries of all that you have – or have not – achieved from your form master, with a final word or two from the headmaster – kindly Mr Cox at Firs Hill Primary School, or broodingly stern HJS Wilson at Firth Park Grammar School – and all read so slowly and solemnly, over the kitchen table, as you stare, anxiously, biting your lip, into the sputtering flames of the fire.

The remarks, from the teachers of your favourite subjects, that make you smile, coyly, with relief. The others, from teachers you have never especially liked or even much listened to, from that seat of yours, so carefully chosen, at the back of the class, swift words of condemnation and curt dismissal, charges of idleness, dreaming, a lack of serious attention. All true, of course.

Yes, suddenly, as if thanks to some malevolent conjuring trick, they all turn up again, in the loft of my mother's house in Totley, where she has kept them safe for almost half a century in a small dapper brown cardboard suitcase once owned by my stepfather. And then, after her death eight years ago, they are transferred to my study in Clapham, South London, where they have been lying in wait, neglected, like long-unsuspected roadside devices, ready and primed to go off all over again.

You count them – thirteen in all! – and then look again at what they said about you then, all those years ago, my goodness. Had their words been strangely prophetic? Did they know, with uncanny accuracy, what you would become? And what of those written so blandly that, surely, they had barely noticed your existence?

There are two interesting remarks about sport which I read with a careless degree of interest because, frankly, I have never been good at sports of any kind. Nor has that fact ever troubled me. At the age of thirteen, after two years at the Grammar School, my sports master tells my mother this: 'still not able to swim'. Brutally dismissive. I feel like telling him – shouting the words into his ear – why that might be so. I feel like grabbing hold of him by the lapels of his jacket, and telling him, to his face, about the cruelty of Mr Scott, the casually sadistic elderly swimming instructor at Sutherland Road Baths, where I had been taken from Firs Hill School as an eight-year-old boy, and how he had insisted that I jump in even though he knew that I could not swim, and how I could not disobey him; and how I thought when I went under, desperately flailing my arms and gulping in water, that I would surely drown, and how I had not, after all, drowned, and had, as a consequence of his brutality, feared swimming ever after. And, to this day, at the age of 68, I am still a lamentably poor and unadventurous swimmer, who finds it unpleasant to have his head anywhere other than above the water, neck craned up like a fowl.

The other remark makes me smile. Again I am at the grammar school, this time eleven years of age and in my first year, and my football teacher has this to say about my behaviour on the pitch: 'Moves too fast for his ability on the soccer field.' I see myself racing hither and thither like a mad eye, wind in my sails, down an unlevel playing field, and seldom engaging with a football. And especially not engaging, on a day of sousing rain and howling wind, with a heavy wet leather football arriving from nowhere at head height.

Of sterner stuff is a statement by my form teacher Miss Windle when I was seven years old and at Firs Hill Primary School: 'Accuracy springs from sound tables.' I say this now to the ghost of Miss Windle: my tables have never been sound, Miss E Windle. Your stern words were never quite heeded. My tables have always been slightly wonky and unsteady.

Sheffield and my mother's curlers

Never a night passed by without my mother going through her usual ritual with those flippin' curlers. Life at Coningsby Road – or, later on, at her house in Totley – would have been unimaginable without it.

The cloudy, well used polythene bag of plastic curlers, all in her favourite colours (purple, pink, blue), which were usually secured shut by means of a runner band, would be waiting at the far corner of the kitchen table, together with a handful of grips, her large blue comb (often none too clean), and an oval hand mirror with a hinged wooden flap at the back, which enabled her to prop the mirror upright directly in front of her fiercely scrutinising face. I used to like that hand mirror. It had a little spray of painted plaster flowers around the top edge.

Ay, there was nothing more unruly than a woman's head hair, and those curlers were waiting there in that bag to do their duty by it. They were strange things, those curlers. I would often pick one up when she was not looking, and examine it. It reminded me of a spare cog from a machine – a clock perhaps – idling away its life in a kind of purposeless limbo. You wanted to put it somewhere, make something work with it. Except that it was plastic, very light when you threw it up and caught it again in your hand, whereas cogs were usually tough and heavy and made of metal, and they didn't come in silly colours.

She would begin by exasperatedly prinking and pushing at lengths of her hair, often sighing disgustedly as she did so. She'd let it fall forward in front of her face like a curtain, half-hiding it, then blow on it through the side of her mouth. Just look at this mess, I ask you, she might say, tut-tutting, I can't do owt with it, as if inviting us all to share in her usual nightly vexation at the state of her hair. No one did so, of course. My grandfather Harold, who, in common with the rest of us, had heard it all before, carried on reading behind the *Sheffield Telegraph*. He might give it a tiny snap as he folded it back in order to drown out her voice. I was usually far too busy sipping at my delicious tumblerful of warm, pre-bedtime cow's milk to bother my head over women's hair and such like.

Having, for the second or third time, picked up a little shank of her hair between thumb and finger, and then let it collapse hopelessly back into its usual slightly stringy lifeless shape, she would determine, once and for all, to do something about it. In fact, she would determine to do what she always did, every night that God sent, to bring it back to some kind of condition of responsiveness.

She'd fish out one of them curlers from the bag with two fingers of one hand, worming her way in to it, pushing it about the table top, without actually looking, and in the other she'd take up a length of her lanky hair, sighing a bit again as she looked at it. Then, getting close enough to that mirror to make it go all foggy, like a road at night, she'd wind the hair tight round the curler.

Holding curler and hair tight in one hand, she'd then take up a grip in the other, and, having opened it up into two little prongs between her teeth, she'd thrust in the grip so that it held the hair in place, curled up tight with the curler. She were always biting her lip when she did that bit. It didn't half take some concentrating. And so, strand by strand, she'd go all over her head until every bit of hair was caught up tight. After that, she'd put a hair net over the top.

When that was done, she'd probably mash a cup of tea, look round the room as if it had never gone away, and even smile a bit. What you looking at when you're at home, mester man? she'd sometimes say if I'd forgotten on purpose to take myself off to bed. Isn't it way past your bedtime? Nothing, I'd say, still thinking about how her skin looked, stretched all taut across her face, and how her head seemed all knobbly and big. More like crags than my mother's head.

They all did it though, women in Fir Vale. They even went out like that, in their curlers, half hidden by a head scarf, to do their shopping. Weekends especially, when they were getting ready for their big night out down the Cannon Hall, Saturday night, when you let your hair down for once and splurged a bit. They looked so ugly though in the day, when they went out like that. It were deliberate though. They knew they were doin' it. They made themselves look ugly in order to look beautiful in the pub later. Once they'd taken that net off, and whipped out the curlers, and combed it all out – feathered it all out more like, with such gentle care – it would still be stuck up there, in its proper place, all tight-curly and lovely. Men folk wouldn't even have noticed that they'd looked ugly when they were making tea in their pinnies and their hair nets. All they'd see was all that beautiful curled hair later. They'd raise their glasses of stout to it, and then another. They might even cheer a bit if they were in a cheering mood that night, if they were flush.

My Grundig Tape Recorder

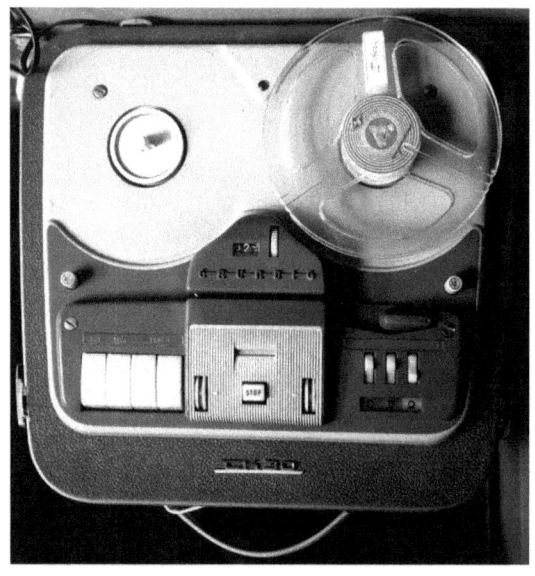

My Grundig reel-to-reel tape recorder was heaved into 45 Coningsby Road in my own proud arms in the spring of 1964, the year that the Beatles played the Ed Sullivan show. I don't remember who I bought it from. Somebody local most likely. It definitely wasn't shop-bought new. Precious little was in those days except long-playing records, which I could buy painlessly, in weekly instalments, through Freeman's, my mother's club. My mother and sister loved going through the fat Freeman's catalogue, poring over pages of dresses and jumpers and shoes, laughing and pointing at the models, the way they were casually walking or posing in their teetering heels. They were forever dreaming about buying new stuff, ordering clothes, and then sending them back by return post (free) because they didn't look quite so good in our kitchen in winter, with the electric light on, as they did in the sun of those photos. One and sixpence a week for about six months, that's what a long-playing record cost by the likes of Del Shannon and Chris Montez – I'd seen both of them at the City Hall by the time I bought the records – by which time the record was scratched to death, and good for nothing except skimming across our back yard.

It was heavy as a tank, that grey Grundig, and built in the shape of a hefty cardboard box. I used to heave it down the stairs on my hip, late on a Sunday afternoon, from the bedroom that I shared with my uncle Ken, so that I could record Alan Freeman's weekly programme of chart toppers on the radio. I knew all about the charts, who was up and who was down. I used to buy *Disc* and *New Musical Express* every week, cut out the current list of top thirty singles, and paste them into a scrap book. So I knew almost as much as Alan Freeman when, hand poised on the record button, I heard his familiar voice saying *Hello pop pickers everywhere!* That's how it always started, that programme.

Forty-five minutes to each side of tape, that's how much music you got. Then, when one side of the tape was full, you had to lift the reels of tape off the spools, turn them over ever so carefully, plonk them back onto the spools, and once again thread the tape through and past the two bits of metal that picked up the music. They were a bit like little fixed magnets to look at, those metal bits that trapped the tape. It could have been boring iron filings you were capturing between them, except it wasn't. It was pop music. It was quite a finicky business though, all that careful lifting and twisting over and re-threading, and sometimes you were daft or careless enough to drop the full reel, and it went bowling over the kitchen floor, yards and yards of thin brown plastic tape, unspooling and unspooling, until it clattered to a stop in the corner by the sink. If it got all twisted and crinkly in the process, it might be useless forever more.

The results were marvellous though, capturing all those chart-topping singles by Gerry and the Pacemakers or the Dave Clark Five or Billy J. Kramer and the Dakotas that now you didn't have to buy, one by one, at Philip Cann's down Chapel Walk, saving all that money.

When I got a bit older, I began to borrow long-playing Argo recordings of poetry being spoken by actors – Milton, Shakespeare, Yeats – from the Central Library, and record them over my old pop hits. I was obviously getting more sophisticated in my tastes. I was also learning to speak poems in a different voice. When I listen to myself reading a poem in my nineteen-year-old voice on one of those old, reel-to-reel tapes, I discover something that shocks me: all that listening to actors speaking poetry on those long-playing records was knocking the Sheffieldish out of me. I was beginning to sound a bit like an actor myself, speaking the Queen's English. Oh god, not her when she's at home!

Local Heroines: Kitty

Kitty was one of life's routines. I never thought much of her really because she was so often at the door of 45 Coningsby Road, wiry, nervy, behatted, chirping like a bird, a very prim and proper spinster lady. My mother usually found those visits exasperating. Although it has to be said that the arrival of human beings at the door were usually a cause for exasperation – unless it happened to be the coal man, heaving a sack across his back, with his slouched cap, coal-dust-blackened face, and flash of white teeth.

She would sigh when she saw Kitty pass by the kitchen window, head bobbing, eager for a bit of company. It's that one again, oh god, she'd say, at her usual cadgin'… Turnin' up like a bad penny. My grandmother took no notice. It was just Dorothy again, having one of her usual rants. And so when Kitty, bright as a button, put her head round the door – she allus did that – Mabel would smile, welcome her in and, having vigorously wiped her hands, back and front, on her pinny, put the kettle on. Dorothy didn't even bother to look up. She knew what to expect, that one again. Not Mabel though. Mabs were always kind hearted. She'd always got time for Kitty. She'd even give a copper to a tramp or a gypsy in exchange for nothing in return.

My mother whipped around her with a duster as Kitty just sat there at the kitchen table in hat and coat, gloved hands wrapped around the warm cup, chatting twenty to the dozen. She was always smartly dressed as if she was going somewhere. She never was. Just down to the shops at Fir Vale Bottom and back. She ate like a bird, my mother said. Too mean to eat owt much, she'd add. The only creature she fed much to was her waddlin' cat, and my mother felt a bit disgusted by that.

I used to stop my bike just to stare at the aspidistra in the window of the front room she kept for best, the dark one that no one ever sat in, with the china cabinet in it you were never allowed to open – you just had to be contented to look through the glass and not fiddle, she allus said – full of funny little precious trinkets and a painted toy house with a lid that came off – she kept coppers in it because it rattled – and a blue glass for a tot of sherry, she said, at Christmas. The house was just like ours in every other respect, three quarters of the way along the road towards the Sunbeam Fish Bar.

That aspidistra plant in the window sat in a big brash blue pot, and its fat lolling leaves shone as if they'd been polished. They had an' all. That was one of Kitty's various weekly routines, washing the aspidistra plant on a Thursday morning. The others were as I'll tell you, and they never changed, week in, week out. That's just how Kitty was. Way, why not though? She'd only got herself to fend for – that said, she had a bit of a hopeless nephew, puffed out, slow movin', sad, rather decrepit lookin' bloke who allus had a long face on, an' who never did owt with his life, and used to come by to borrow money. Sad what happened to him in the end. Or rather what didn't. When he pulled the mattress off of her bed after she'd passed away – nearly brought on a hernia just doin' it – he found all those piles of ten shilling notes in rubber bands. She'd scrooged them away for too long though. Not one of them was valid. That put paid to his dreams. She didn't do it on purpose though. Nobody trusted banks. Cash should be kept by you for a rainy day or it might just vanish into thin air. An' it did if you left it there long enough.

Kitty's Weekly Routine

Monday was always wash day, which meant that all the clothes went through a vigorous dunking in the dolly tub, followed by an extra scrub on the table top in the kitchen. After this the mangle took over. Once through was never enough. The process had to be repeated at least three more times. Finally, out would come the old clothes horse. It was huge, and it would be draped with combinations, bloomers, vests, camisoles – everything always looked so big.

Tuesday was market day, mainly shopping for the cat, very little for her. All the meat stalls at the market would be scoured for cat lites, for which she only paid a few coppers (tinned cat meat was unheard of in those days). She would proudly call in on us on the way back to show us what she'd got for fourpence. Out of the bag she'd produce two parcels wrapped in newspaper, each one containing lumps of vile smelling and even more repulsive looking animal intestines. Once back home, she'd get the pot on the boil, filling the house with a horrible aroma. Finally cooked, the offending lumps would be impaled on hooks and hung on a line in the kitchen, with only the cat making mews of approval.

Wednesday was upstairs day. You could always see her sitting on the window sill, cleaning the outside of the windows. Everybody else paid a window cleaner to do this, but not Kitty. Carpets and dusters were vigorously shaken out of the window, floor scrubbed and polished, bed changed. She didn't have any furniture other than a bed and an old wooden chair that was falling to bits. In the other bedroom, which was tiny, she had a mattress on the floor. This is where her nephew would sleep when he occasionally stayed with her for the night. This didn't happen very often, but the usual routine had to be followed. The mattress would be brought down and beaten to within inches of its life, and the floor underneath it scrubbed clean.

Thursday was the day when the front room was cleaned. Four aspidistra plants were carried out into the back yard. After a thorough washing, they were left standing by the grate to drain. Each leaf was carefully polished until it shone. This room also contained an old, three-piece, horsehair suite that had once belonged to her mother. It was too full of holes to sit on. She used to dress it up with a dilapidated dust sheet. That front room also boasted a small bamboo table, on which were carefully stacked a handful of women's journals, dated from around the year dot. When Thursday's tasks were completed to her satisfaction, Kitty would sit down to a meagre tea of bread and jam. The cat would be standing on the table at her elbow, greedily eating a pile of lites cut from the lump in the corner.

Friday was dedicated to the cleaning of the kitchen, after which she would carefully draw across her very threadbare curtains, fill the bowl in the sink, and have a strip wash and a complete change of underclothes. Friday afternoon would find her in the market once again, buying a tiny joint of meat for the weekend, followed by a rummage through a second-hand stall from which she bought all her clothes.

Saturday was spent in Firth Park for the most part, sitting around the bowling green, chatting to whoever would listen. She would wear her Sunday best for this occasion because it was undoubtedly the highlight of her week. Wherever it was possible, she would walk. She would not take a bus or a tram. My mother always said that she begrudged spending the money.

Sunday was cooking day. The joint of meat went into the oven first. This was followed by a small fruit loaf, and then an apple pie. It was the one day of the week when she indulged herself. It has to be said that she made very nice pastry and cakes. Her working life had been spent in a bakehouse.

Thus ended Kitty's weekly routine.

The Pain and the Glory of Shopping in Sheffield

'The Gates of Heaven' by the wonderful Pete McKee

Life's brief catalogue of near overwhelming dullnesses as a teenager included the horror of shopping for other people's clothes, my mother's, my sister's. To stand outside any big Sheffield department store in the 1960s – C & A in Fargate, or Debenhams or Pauldons down the Moor – as disgruntled as any tethered dog, waiting for my mother and my sister to emerge, sweating, laughing, excitable, talking twenty to the dozen, heaving their large bags of fripperies after them, was as exquisite a torment as any footloose teenager might not wish for. And then to have to help carry the stuff, on tram or bus, before dumping it onto the table top in the kitchen at Coningsby Road with a sigh of disgust, and to disappear upstairs, quick as a flash, back to the close companionship of a book, in order to avoid all the chit chat about the marvels of this flowery dress or that pretty, flimsy, sparkly top.

Occasionally to have to suffer the boredom and the humiliation of standing in that tall, grim, featureless box of a changing room, having whipped the curtain back across to keep out my mother's helpful prying eyes, and then to prepare myself to drag around my unwilling bony shoulders yet another brown or green corduroy jacket, always stiff and cold to the touch, or to yank, fast, up my boring, spindly legs a draughty pair of trousers in a similar range of dull, soul-sapping colours, and watch the long mirror reflect the disgust in my face, which always bordered on downright opposition.

And to recognise now that this attitude was the cause of why, in those early teenage years and even on, I was the epitome of stylelessness, and why girls took that view too, which often made me miserable to be with and miserable on my own. Why could I not take a cue from my sister's boy friend Haydn, who flashed through our house like a brilliant comet, with comb ever at the ready, slicked-back hair, winklepickers, and even slicker drainpipe trousers?

Yes, clothes were a side-issue, an irrelevance, a means to an end, which was to conceal one's nakedness, and nothing more than that.

My mother wanted me to look respectable above all things else, and I had no interest in resisting her, so when on holiday in Blackpool, shameful images of myself show me walking at her side in my school uniform or, a little older, in sports jacket and tie, as if I were a very young husband in the making, utterly docile and conventional. Why was I not alive in the swinging 60s? Or did that happen a little later? To me, never. Well, perhaps right at the end, after I had left Sheffield to go to university. It was then that I began to break out into blue loons and sloppy mohair sweaters.

I blame religion in part. Religion had to do with inward happiness, and never with outward display, which signified nothing of value at all, and ran in fact counter to God's purposes. Outward display meant vanity, which was to be avoided at all costs.

And yet there was one moment of the year, as a child, when I looked forward to shopping, and one big shop – yes, one alone – that I would speed to like an arrow let loose from a bow: Redgates down the Moor, on the same side as Suggs for your sportsgear...

Redgates, which sold toys of every description, was a child's paradise, and there was no better place to be escorted to by your mother in the weeks of rising and rising excitement just before Christmas. Even its name had such an allure. Red was my favourite colour, and a gate was a thing to be flung open, onto a field where you could run and run and run...

Children walked and danced and jigged and spun round in a drunken dream in that place, buying everything that their eyes fell upon, from Ack-Ack guns with their plastic yellow nozzle ends that pulsed in and out to the accompaniment of a deafening racket when you squeezed the trigger, to the latest Hornby 00 Trains, complete with miles of tracks that seemed to wind in and out right around the shop. There were cardboard bins with higglety-pigglety mounds of small, soft toys through which you could run your hands, model Spitfires, already, as if by some miracle, made up from their balsa wood parts and painted in their fighting wartime colours, suspended from wires and bearing down on you at dangerous angles. There were also scooters, bikes, trolleys – the lot...

There was also a Dan Dare hand puppet, with rubbery head and green cloth body, into which you pushed your fingers to make his features move, and a cap on the top of his head to make him look smart and in charge of the galaxy, which was what I got. That was my big Christmas treat.

To the Moor

A toast to its coming resurrection as the shoppers' paradise

Down this gently sloping street,
Down this mecca of old-fashioned shopping pleasures,
Let my feet go tripping and skipping.
Let old shillings jangle in my pocket
And new notes come spilling.

Let me say those names over to myself –
Pauldons, Atkinsons, Roberts, Redgates –
As I dart into first one and then another, ever singing.
Oh glorious palaces of bygone enchantment,
You who hold out to me forever
Promises of new coats, and ever sheerer stockings!

And when I mount the bus back, weary, to Pitsmoor,
Laden like a mule with bags in abundance –
Too many to be carried, yet still I carry them –
Toys for the kiddies, a new coat for mother,
A trilby for father…

I ask you, O Moor ever more-ish,
To stay vivid in my heart and my mind forever.
(And forgive us, o furious father, for the damage to the pocket.)

Big Girls

Some of the girls are just
too big for my liking.
They're too noisy an all,
like fog horns blaring.

I like the smaller ones
with the quiet voices,
the ones who don't run at you
in the playground,
pretending not to notice.

Big girls take up too much space
in the classroom.
They always know what's what,
even when they don't.

I'm never going to love a girl
that's six inches taller than I am
in her stockinged feet.
I'm not partial
to being frowned down on.

Our Modest Bookcase at 45 Coningsby Road

I did not begin to acquire book-shelving of my own until I was about sixteen years old. By that time, the population of our terraced house in Fir Vale house was beginning to thin out. My sister Pat had married Haydn in spite of my mother's disapproval of his social inadequacies; my Uncle Ken had moved up into the world of Broomhill by marrying Aunt Ena; and my grandmother Mabel was already ailing, uncomplainingly. She would die in 1967. That left myself, my mother and my grandfather. We had halved in numbers.

At the age of sixteen, I moved upstairs to the attic. A door was built at the bottom of the twisty flight of stairs which led up to it. I had a room of my own at last. I was sealed off, self-sufficient, free to dream. The walls were wall-papered a deep blue. Although it was at the top of the house, it felt like an undersea world of exquisite, drifting set-apartness. And there, along the long wall that faced the skylight, my mother paid a carpenter to build book-shelving that stretched the entire width of the room. I felt nearly breathless with excitement at the sight of it there. I ran my finger along the shelves, almost fetishistically. I already owned enough books to fill half of the shelving. Most of these were books by Christian commentators. Secular books – poetry, fiction, philosophy – would soon be in eager competition for my attention.

Best of all

Best of all is this attic room
where you shut yourself away
with books and thoughts and biscuits
and read poetry by Shelley
until you fall asleep,
fully-clothed...
Best of all is this attic room
with a skylight corner
from which to see
grey-tiled rooftops
and to hear machinery whining

from that little factory
where you never go,
but glimpse, side-on,
as you hurry up Herries Road
once in a while...

Best of all is to be up here
dreaming of what might be,
and never to go down there
into that hell of stupid talking –
that kitchen of blazing lights,
bustling bodies and reeking bacon –
about nothing that really matters.

It is difficult to understate quite how much books meant to me then, at the very beginning of my life as a writer: the buying of them at Ward's the Booksellers down Chapel Walk, the reading of them, the appreciation of them as wonderfully savoursome and near sacred repositories of knowledge. To have a book in print was the ambition of every writer, and it was no easy matter. There were no self-publishing suites in the 1960s. To be published was a tremendous honour, an indication that a writer had reached a certain level of distinction. Every writer aspired to be published, to show off a book written by himself as final proof of his credibility.

These days knowledge proliferates in so many different ways. The consequence of these changes is that books have an increasingly uncertain status in the life of our society. Second-hand bookshops have virtually disappeared from our streets altogether. When you see one, you discover that its owner almost always looks harried, on the edge, semi-impoverished. Millions grow up these days without even cherishing the idea of the book. This was not the case in the 1960s. In the 1960s books were still reverenced. They were primary sources of knowledge. We went to fat encyclopaedias for our facts, and to our hefty dictionaries to remind ourselves what words meant, and how to spell them correctly. If we were what is now described as dyslexic – there was no such known condition in those days – we were smacked about the head and told to try harder. And where did we most often *find* such books? In public libraries, which were also granted a respect that they no longer possess. Now libraries aspire to be social hubs, complete with easy chairs and atria for daydreaming as the tender fatherly hand rhythmically nudges the handle of the pushchair. No visit to a library is complete without a cup of coffee and a conversation with one's neighbour. Unthinkable once. What is more, the books in local libraries seemed more serious then. Now we are largely expected to dine off cookbooks and other light-weight frivolities.

When did books first get a grip on me? In the wake of my dramatic conversion to Christianity, at a Pioneer Camp in Anglesey, when I was thirteen years old. Until that time, I had had relatively little time for them. I had been a reader – *Jennings*, the *Famous Five*, that sort of thing – but not an impassioned one. After I had pledged my heart to Jesus, I began to recognise that books might be the key to the kingdom of spiritual enlightenment.

There had been relatively few books at 45 Coningsby Road. The family's single workaday bookcase (you can see a crude charcoal drawing of it by my thirteen-year-old hand at the head of this chapter) was painted yellow – had my grandfather made it? That was perfectly possible – and it sat high on a wall, just beside the back door, in the kitchen, that small room where everything of any consequence happened: cooking, eating, arguing, strip-washing at the sink, listening to Workers' Playtime on the radio, doing one's history essay or puzzling over the various possible meanings of a long poem by W.B. Yeats.

Beneath that single shelf of books there were four little drawers in which odds and ends were stored – a thimble, for example, or a miniature pair of scissors. The drawers were far too small to contain anything other than odds and ends. Why so high though? you may be asking yourself. So that the meddlesome fingers of children could not tamper. I remember often looking up at it, suspended there in the air, way beyond my reach. It was very narrow, and it consisted of a single row of shelves.

So much for the bookcase in our kitchen. The mouth-watering prospect of the presence of books in a room of one's own was quite a different matter. As I have mentioned, the importance of books first seized hold of me when I became a

Christian. I knew that I needed them. I bought commentaries on the Bible, books of Christian uplift, different translations of the Old and the New Testament.

By the time I was sixteen years old, everything had changed. I had book shelving of my own. I began to feel as if I was living in a library, and the surrounding presence of so many books became, little by little, a source of security. It also contributed to my feelings of self-worth. I began to feel that to own a book was almost the equivalent of having read, understood and profited by it. Books also acted as a kind of barricade against the world. I felt stockaded inside all that knowledge, bolstered, encouraged, given strength and presence. I knew that visitors would be impressed by my library, that they would assume a depth of reading and understanding merely by scanning the titles on my shelves. All that was immensely self-satisfying. (I did read them, of course.) Some of them are on my shelves here in Clapham today: those wonderful anthologies by Lagarde & Michard that seemed to offer exhaustive accounts of great French literature of the seventeenth, nineteenth and twentieth centuries. How I still love those hardback books, with their marvellous illustrations: André Gide, sage-like in his fez, or a photograph of an extraordinary painting by Yves Tanguy, which began to open up to me the alternative reality of surrealism, and was undoubtedly one of the first images which set me off seriously dreaming about the art of the twentieth century.

Harold's Book

John Harris' *Covenant with Death* was one of the few books that I remember my family ever owning during my Sheffield years, and it lived in that small bookcase of a single shelf, no more than a foot and a half in width, that was positioned high on the wall, well beyond the reach of the fingers of meddling children, in our often hot and fuggy kitchen just a couple of feet from the stove and the kitchen table. This book was something of a revered object. It sat wedged there, protected by standard brown wrapping paper of the kind that was more generally used to send off a parcel to a friend, and it kept company with Charles Dickens' *A Tale of Two Cities* (which my grandfather would dutifully read once a year), a small dictionary, my uncle's copy of Fowler's *Modern English Usage*, and probably a selection of books – historical romances by the likes of Jean Plaidy and Georgette Heyer – borrowed by my mother that week from Firth Park Library.

My grandfather enlisted with the Sheffield City Battalion along with many of his friends and neighbours. That battalion suffered terrible losses at the Somme. About five hundred had gone to war. Fewer than a dozen returned. My grandfather said nothing about this war during my lifetime with the exception of a pleasantry about his ill-judged comic efforts to buy chickens from a local farmer, always re-told in ill-pronounced, pidgin French, and accompanied by ridiculous, jabbing-finger gestures – like an inverted v-sign. *Deux comme ça!* was the standard phrase, which is still imprinted on my memory. That story was re-told at the drop of a hat. It was a kind of party piece. In this way were terror and misery kept safely locked away in its box.

John Harris, a local novelist born in Rotherham, had paid a visit to our house in Coningsby Road one day in the early 1960s – it was quite an event to have an illustrious stranger (he was also a feature writer on the *Rotherham Advertiser*) come calling on official business – to interview my grandfather Harold about a novel Harris was researching about the Great War. What exactly did Harold tell John Harris? He never let us know, and when, many years later, killing time on a train between Sheffield and London St Pancras, I combed the book itself for clues, there were none to be found. Perhaps Harold's confidences on that day had been used to give atmosphere, leaven the whole, nothing more than that. There was no trace of the man I had known as my maternal grandfather.

A few months ago, staying with my older sister in Holymoorside, a village just outside Chesterfield, I came across an old, badly creased sepia photograph from 1914. In fact, it is a photograph in the form of a post card, a memorial to be sent on to others. It shows a group of twenty young soldiers from the Sheffield Battalion at a training camp as they prepare to go off to war. They are posed in two rows, one seated, the other standing, in front of a long wooden hut made from slatted wood. It is quite a casual shot. Some of the young men are smiling into the camera. Others sit side-on, legs crossed. One boy has his arm around the shoulders of another. My grandfather is standing in the back row, clean-shaven, serious-looking, abundant black hair swept straight back from his forehead. He would always sweep it back in that way.

My grandfather has inscribed many of these individual portraits with a single letter, in blue ink from his fountain pen – it is the same hand on the back, where the words read: 'Some of the Lads at Redmires Camp, Nov 1914'. There are three different letters: K, W, M. Six of them are marked with a K, five with a W, and just one with an M. The meaning is not difficult to come by: six of them died, five were wounded (goodness knows how badly) and one went missing. A combined toll of death or wounding of sixty per cent. John Harris barely disguises the name of this camp in his novel. He calls it Blackmires, turning red to black in some kind of grim acknowledgement of the aftermath of that most foolish and deadly of wars.

Another glimpse of my grandfather Harold Hickson, veteran of the Somme

You could have set a clock by my grandfather's habits – breakfast at eight, dinner at one, tea at five, supper by nine. For breakfast, he would cook his own bacon and mushrooms, laying out the food on a plate on the kitchen table just before he went to bed, and then carefully covering it with a saucer against flies. At breakfast he would crozzle those mushrooms in the frying pan until they looked as hard and as small as the fragments of shrapnel which were still said to lodge in his lower leg. I have certainly stared at some curious bumps in my time. His stockings were kept in place by leather supports, buttonable, which you only spotted when he crossed his legs. His wardrobe, which was impressively large and wide-ranging, included a pair of stretchy silver arm bands which held up the rolled sleeves of his shirts. When he went out in his sports jacket of muted colour, a white handkerchief would always be lolling, fetchingly, from its breast pocket.

After breakfast, he would wrench his mac down from his own hook at the bottom of the steep flight of stairs that led directly up to the bedrooms, hang a stout walking stick over his arm, and go for his daily constitutional. 'I'm just going round the lump, Doff,' were his familiar words before leaving. A cup of Nescafé after that, prepared by my ever willing mother Dorothy.

Hs more formal wear was saved for the seaside, and for Blackpool Promenade in particular. There he would sit on a wooden bench facing the sea, seldom looking at my grandmother, who would be seated beside him, part-hidden beneath her straw hat, and equally grimly resigned of demeanour. I seldom remember any laughter which was not of my own making. It was usually at their expense. The sun would be blazing overhead, and they would be dressed as if for the onset of autumn or winter in some place ever censoriously mindful of its strict dress code. Meanwhile, smeared across the great expanse of golden beach below them, small, near-naked children would be shouting and squirming like eels in the sand. My grandfather, meanwhile, would be staring out to sea, tongue slow-lapping a cone of vanilla ice cream that would be furled in his breast-pocket handkerchief.

In old age, he would climb those steep stairs up to the bedrooms at 45 Coningsby Road in a pair of old house slippers that badly needed some mending. He was, life-long, his own mender, custodian of the black Singer sewing machine, but this time, thanks to his ailing eyes, he had done a bad job. And yet, being stubborn as a mule, he still insisted, crossly, that they were right as rain. They were not right as rain. Having reached the top of the stairs, he missed his footing and fell back down, swallowing his tongue, and precipitating, in time, a haemorrhage that would lead to his death. My mother stared in horror at the golf ball that had grown, as if by some miracle of compressed time, at the back of his head.

He was entirely in the grip of his own rigid routines. And others were obliged to taper the shapes of their lives to fit in with his. Or else. There was simply no alternative. The older he became, the more exacting and tyrannical his behaviour. I tiptoed around him, fearing his displeasure. We were always at a tangent to each other.

Sheffield Royal Infirmary

The Victorian buildings of Sheffield were always frowningly black and heavy-looking in those distant days of the 1950s and 1960s. Many of them had survived the war. Others had been terribly damaged, and now thrust themselves up into the air like rotten, broken teeth. Yet others would not survive the peace of the wrecker's ball that came swinging in the aftermath of those dark years of conflict. They brooded over you, those grand civic piles. They seemed to reprimand you for your shortcomings, your levity. They were all about officialdom, and a kind of grimly overbearing seriousness, never about movement, friskiness, youthfulness or laughter. They held you to account. They boxed you in. They demanded good behaviour.

Industrial pollution was to blame for their darkness, at least in part. We who grew up in the 1950s could never have imagined that a Victorian building could be golden in colour, beautifully fair, light on its feet. That was only to emerge years later, after the passage of the Clean Air Act of 1956, when the best of them were cleaned – Sheffield Town Hall, for example – and they were at last able to throw off decades of grime and pollution – like coquettish young women making a splash at a ball. At last, soot would stop falling from the air onto the washing in the back yard. My mother heaved a sigh of relief – no more bed sheets to be whisked in before they got ruined by those specks of white snow!

Perhaps that forbidding blackness is why, in part, those buildings were so unloved or disregarded, and why concrete, which, when new, looks so fair and so light by comparison, was so readily and so easily embraced. It seemed to belong to us, that material. It was fast and easily manipulable, clean-lined and unfussy. As quick to assemble as Bayko. It seemed to speak of the now. Black Victorian buildings, with all their strangely finicky detailing, seemed like an oppressive reminder of all that was rapidly passing away.

The Sheffield Royal Infirmary was one of those buildings. It was enormous in size, black and indomitable, and it existed at the bottom of one of Sheffield's steepest and longest streets, Rutland Road, which hurtled, straight and swift as an arrow, down from Pitsmoor and into the valley's bottom.

And there it stood, that antique, colonnaded late eighteenth-century hospital, waiting to embrace the sick and those who tended on them. I experienced it at first hand, twice, and at quite different periods of my life, as a helpless and frightened child, and then, more than a decade later, as a broody, inward-looking, bookish youth on the brink of university. As a child, I had my tonsils removed. In those days the operation was done almost as a matter of course, in order to prevent infection. The thinking is a little different now. Most children are allowed to keep their tonsils. I also worked there as a porter after I had left school.

The tonsillectomy was a matter of being taken, firmly, on the bus by my mother, and then left in an alien place. There was little conversation about what exactly was going to happen to me. My mother was always quite vague about these things, and nervous and over-respectful of doctors. She was trying to distract me, I felt, as we made that journey, hand in hand. Perhaps she was also trying to distract herself from feeling the pain of being away from me. I remember her promising me a toy car from Mr Brown's down Owler Lane at the end of it. It was the first time that I had been left overnight on my own.

That night I lay in a ward that seemed bigger than almost any other room that I had ever seen. I felt so small and so cold in the bed that I had been given. It was autumn, and the days were drawing in. In my memory, the ward in which I lie is almost lightless. Well perhaps there is a strange greenish light, but even that is dying away as I look and look towards the window. Some distance away other bodies are lying, shuffling, sniffling, turning restlessly, crying. There is no conversation.

Then, in my memory, I cut to my mother's return, of her bursting through a pair of swing doors in her big green winter overcoat with the checked patterning, of breathing the cool, fresh air of the out-of-doors, and our homeward journey. All that strange hospital stillness and frozenness has gone. There is a tremendous bustle of freedom – noise, idle chatter – everywhere. Vehicles are zipping past in a kind of holiday mood. The road is slick and shiny in the aftermath of cooling rain.

We are being happily jostled around downstairs on the bus. It is as if the bus is playing games with us, throwing us first left and then right, to celebrate my return from hospital. Even the bus conductor smiles when he turns the handle of the machine, and hands over the little squarish tickets that roll out from it. My throat feels strange, stiff and numb, not quite mine any more, but I am happy all the same. I have been released. I am on my way to a red sportscar, a Dinky toy, from Mr Brown's down Owler Lane. I am skipping in front of my mother, higher and higher, and she is laughing at my daft antics.

Years later, I return to the Sheffield Royal Infirmary in a quite different guise. Now I am no longer a small, frightened and bewildered child. I am a much more self-assured and self-absorbed young man, head crammed with book-learning and fragments of half-written poems, who is preparing himself to go to university, and I am racing down Rutland Road on my drop-handle-barred bike, that precious Sun *Soleil d'Or*, head held meanly low, all wind-raked hair, in an excitable hurry, about to begin my six weeks of work as a hospital porter.

The uniform is a long, dowdy brown, sloppily-fitting coat with, handily, pockets that will take a book or two – or a pair of hands on a cold day when those hands are not otherwise engaged. My greatest wish – shared by everyone else, of course – is to spend as much time as possible out of harm's way in the low-ceilinged, subterranean porters' lodge, with its metal lockers, saggy old armchairs, garishly intrusive central light bulb, and hob on which a kettle seems to be on the boil, permanently. There are older men who have been there for years and know the ropes; know, for example, not to respond too quickly or too eagerly when the black telephone suddenly shrills, which always means: Porter! Porter! Quick! We all look at each other when that happens and then eventually one of us sighs and pushes himself up out of his chair. The others quickly return to their newspapers or books.

They are quite a crew. I spend little time talking to them and a long time observing them, wondering whether they will make good material for a story. Most of them are my senior by several decades. This job is everything that they will ever aspire to, so the game is played long and slow. I admire the somnolent style of Paddy, for example, a kindly, soft-voiced

Irishman with a rather large head, which he often supports in his cupped hands, as if it is a little too melancholy heavy to be borne unsupported for too long. Paddy is in love with being at ease when at work, and of never standing in the way when others are hurtling to take command of any given situation. Yes, Paddy is the artful, watchful foot solder. His voice is gentle and comically murmurous. He has an air of slightly world-weary resignation. When he leaves at the end of his shift, he places on his balding head, at a very particular angle, a rather smart hat, and that gesture and that hat seem to lend him a surprisingly new identity altogether. He has inveigled himself into the world of dapperness. Now he is a man preparing to stride out in the direction of an existence on life's glittering surface, which will clearly demand a little more of him. And, having mustered his energies by lying low all day, he will be ready to respond. Even a woman, flicking her skirt, may hove into view. Almost anything is possible. Paddy has re-invented himself.

And then there is the leader of the porters' pack – there is always one – Jim, who has a very particular job, which he relishes. Goodness knows why. When he bursts back into the lodge after completing a job, his cry, as he wrings his hands, is always the same: *anybody mashin'?* That cry is so comically raucous – it is almost a fairground holler – that we all smile and glance in his direction. Everyone's mood is lifted. Even I look up from my book, keeping my finger in the page. We prepare ourselves to be entertained. At which point, he grabs up the loose tea and the brown tea pot, sets the mashin' process in motion as he sings at the top of his voice, and perhaps even does a little dance.

You cannot but enjoy Jim's company. He so looks the part, almost end-of-pierish, in his scruffy, tight black waistcoat, black spectacles, and the slicked-back sheen of his well oiled black hair, which rides so smoothly over and round the large boil – or perhaps it is a cyst – at the back of his head. He is tumultuously small and always effervescing with stories, and never more so than when he has just finished that favourite job of his – which is to be the principal incinerator shoveller, just next to the mortuary.

It's a demonic place, that brick incinerator, though it looks humdrum enough. A great brick chimney thrusts one hundred feet high into the sky beside it, carrying away the noxious fumes into the upper regions, thank goodness. When Jim is working in front of it, in wellington boots, hefty gloves, biker's goggles and belted mac, heaving his shovel, the incinerator door hangs open, flames eagerly lapping like a greedy tongue, to receive everything that he is ready to heave into it, and he always does so with great gusto. All the rubbish to be dealt with is heaped up around it in untidy, mightily unhygienic heaps – from cardboard boxes with used syringes spilling out, to assorted human limbs (wrapped). The flames roar with greedy delight as Jim flings it all in, laughing and warbling as he goes.

Meanwhile, I see myself standing next to the door of the mortuary, one hand on a metal trolley, having just made a delivery, watching him, smiling at him toiling away so cheerily at hell's mouth.

What did I do all day at that place? The principal tasks included pushing canisters of oxygen around from store to ward, deftly twisting and manoeuvring them up and onto iron trolleys with rubber wheels, and then bowling along the corridor until I reached the ward, where a patient would be waiting, head usually turned to the side, with heaving chest, desperate for air.

There was little or no human contact between medical staff and porter. We were cogs in a machine, barely worth more than a second's glance. After acknowledging a curt nod of acceptance, I would leave again, with clanky empty canister, a considerably lighter burden, and when out of eyeshot I would put on speed in order to reward myself with a little light entertainment.

The second common task was the solemn removal of the sheet-wrapped bodies. This happened most often during the night. The night-time hours were the hours of death and, somehow, that seemed right. It would require two of us to do the job, one at the head end and another at the foot. Having lifted the body, we would let it settle, gently, onto the often rickety feeling metal trolley, and then we would pull it, with all due solemnity, along the floor of the sleeping, light-dimmed ward and out of the door. Once out into the yard between the buildings with its blast of cold night air, our pace would quicken mightily. In fact, we would dare each other to run, gathering pace, screeching around corners – until we reached the mortuary.

Once indoors, one of us would swing open one of those great, long fridge doors and, inhaling a sudden throat-catching blast of cold air, pull out an empty rolling metal shelf. There would always be one empty shelf. You could count on it. The wrapped corpse would be deposited there, and then, having rolled it back into the chill, we would swing the great door slam shut to the accompaniment of a satisfying hollow boom.

After that, came tea and a book in the Lodge and, if we were lucky, a bit of shut eye. The mortician often spent time with us in the porters' lodge. I could never understand why. Could he be that lowly a personage? He was a fairly young man, with a serious moustache and well tended hair, who always behaved soberly, as if he had lessons to teach us that would surely drag us back from our addiction to lives of unremitting frivolity. Lessons in life and death perhaps, the thin line that divides the one from the other. He was not much older than me, but there was a great gulf of experience between us, his grave demeanour always seemed to be suggesting.

I preferred the night shift above all others. There was little talk in the lodge at nights. Most porters preferred to sleep. There was almost no social life either, no light chit chat to be heard, as you roamed the near empty corridors of the hospital, snooping around corners like a ghost. You could be almost wholly alone with your drifting thoughts at night. You could even write down those significant thoughts in a notebook to your heart's content. The big black telephone on that shelf in the Lodge was much more shrill and jarring in the night though – it seemed much more urgent a sound altogether when darkness pressed its face against the window. More akin to a police siren. It also seemed more offensive, as if it was trying to catch us out in our idleness. Which was true, of course.

I always enjoyed leaving the hospital at dawn, just after sunrise. The streets were empty, and although it was a fearfully difficult and long climb back up Rutland Road to Pitsmoor, standing up in the saddle as I pushed down on the pedals nearly all the way, there was the promise of sleep in a morning of daylight, which was always very pleasing. I was contented to be slumbering in my bed against the grain, to be walking in one direction when the rest of the world was walking in the other. It felt like the sort of thing that a youth with ambitions to be a writer whose task it was to beam a sharp light on the antics of the world should be doing.

There is also something to be said for a modicum of weary cheerfulness.

Writing, Words and Silence: the lesson of Stanley Cook

Stanley Cook

There was very little silence in our house at Coningsby Road until I acquired a room of my own at the age of sixteen. Then I was able, having closed shut the door to the attic which had become my study, to create a room full of nothing but silence. Then that silence could become marvellously deafening. Out of that silence voices would emerge. Some of them would sound like many of the voices that I had always known and spent my life listening to, for better or for worse – my uncle's voice, my grandfather's, my mother's. I would hear them ringing in my head all over again. I would rehearse, to my heart's content, their words, decide what exactly they had meant by what they said – what they *really* meant by what they said. Because spoken words are often very slippery things. My relatives spoke vehemently, impulsively, loudly. They spoke in order to make themselves heard, to hear themselves speaking, making great shapes in the air. Words were a form of weaponry. My mother and my grandfather used to joust with words for hours at a time, denouncing each other, pouring scorn on each other, accusing each other of this, that and the other.

As a small child, I used to marvel at all this brutish verbal sparring, rendered all the more dramatic by the tiny space in which all this warfare happened; a species of utterly futile warfare, of course, which, eventually, ended nowhere; ended, in fact, in a kind of wearied collapse into sullen silence. Had one convinced the other of anything? Had anything changed as a result of this indiscriminate verbal warfare? Nothing, it seemed to me. They would take up their cudgels again on another day, re-invigorated by sleep and the fact that they had been bodily set apart from each other for several hours. The same words would come out again, as if fresh-minted, and they would be deployed with the same degree of carelessly carefree bullish vehemence. They would level the same accusations at each other. And the outcome would be exactly the same. Stalemate. There was no victor, ever. It was a pointless, endless war of attrition.

As I listened and listened, utterly fascinated, over the years, I began to draw various conclusions. The most important was this one: surely words deserve better than this. They do not merely exist to be carelessly tossed about the room like house bricks. They deserve more of those who use them. Little by little, I discovered that words need not be treated so badly, and that there were even those – writers, and even some talkers – who reverenced them and used them well. I needed to get to know some of those people. I also needed to learn to use words cleanly and clearly myself so that I never found myself involved in the kind of pointless, mind-numbing skirmishing to which I had so often been a witness at 45

Coningsby Road. What a hopelessly idealistic task I had set myself! I must try all the same.

I soon discovered that words were well used in some books, though not in all books. You had to be as discriminating about books as people. There were slovenly books that hung around cussing on street corners just as there were people who did the same. How to find people who used words well, tactfully, and with discrimination? Were there any local wordsmiths whom I might come to admire? Yes, there was at least one.

So much of the way I speak and think was the accidental gift of one diffident man whose company I fell into almost by chance, at Firth Park Grammar School. He was a poet called Stanley Cook. I have written about him elsewhere, so I shall limit what I say here to just a few remarks. Stanley taught me that words do not have to be raucous. They do not have to be launched like missiles. They do not need to pulverise like bombs. They can be chosen with hesitant discrimination, one by one, so that each one can be savoured to the full for its meaning content. That is how Stanley talked, and it is how he taught me to talk. He taught me that it is not necessary to increase the volume of one's voice in order to get one's point across – in fact, raising the voice is more often than not counter-productive because no one likes to be harangued. To be harangued makes the listener bristle.

English Teacher walking up Barnsley Road, 1967

A stony, bookish man. A life apart
From all the other lives along that street.
A man in a black coat in summertime.
A man pernickety with single leaves.
A stary, bookish man, sparing of words.
A man who nodded when he thought to nod.

At other times, some studied sideways glance
At walls, flowers, trees. Or inward, to some god.
A bookish man, unneighbourly, tall, dour,
Who let his washing hang there, rain or shine.
A man forever walking through these parts,
Swinging a leather bag, shapeless with age.

Writing

Writing is an addiction. It seizes hold of you, and it is difficult to shake off. After you have written regularly for some years, in notebooks, diaries or on odd scraps of used paper – it really does not matter where – you gradually find that you cannot exist without it because it has become a way of explaining your own life to your self, and of making sense of the world. And this is especially the case if you are not very talkative, if you are more interested in listening to other people talk than talking yourself.

Writing can also be a substitute for talking. It is a way of explaining what you think. It is a way of proving to yourself that you are thinking something when other people are waiting for your reply, and they receive nothing in return but silence. That has often happened. I have disappointed or angered people by my silence. I have left them bemused and frustrated. I have not given back to them what they expected to receive. Instead, I have written down what I might have said, but much later, and for the eyes of myself alone.

One of the reasons for this disabling hesitation when in the company of others is that I always feel that I need to prepare my words before speaking them out loud. Like an actor of sorts perhaps. Just speaking is simply not enough. That can lead to careless and superficial talk. Not always though. Of course, some people, even people who genuinely have something to say, talk too much. They don't care that you don't want to go on listening and listening. They don't care that you would rather walk away and catch the next bus home. They talk themselves out. They have nothing inside but what they have just said. By talking, they have empted themselves out like a sack, up-ended all the contents. There was not as much as what they thought in that sack.

I began to write, compulsively, at about the age of fifteen. I could not stop bad poems pouring out of me like water from a tap. I wrote them everywhere, and at all times of the day or night, non-stop effusions. Why poems though? Because poets dealt, strangely, with inner worlds of the self, worlds of feeling. It was not bald descriptive writing that I was after. I had no compelling wish to describe merely what I saw with my own eyes or to create characters that might speak for me. I needed something which would be both inward and outward simultaneously. It needed to be a kind of writing which would serve to explain to myself – yes, I was largely writing in order to talk to myself – what exactly was happening to me as a growing boy-becoming-man who had had his inner world turned upside down by Christianity. The poems improved, little by little, when Christianity began to loosen its grip on me.

My Haunted Mother

My mother, though a mistress of the ungentle art of brutish domestic confrontation when standing staunch in her floral pinny, legs spread, hands on hips, in our straitened, overheated kitchen at Coningsby Road, found meeting strangers a near insuperable burden.

She was always suspicious and unwelcoming. She did not possess general conversational skills. She was visibly cowed, overawed when in the company of others. And then, having listened in silence, she was quick to bad-mouth them later, to twist their words, to find slights in what they had said or more general reasons for believing that they had wronged her. To shun them then seemed like satisfying justice. The truth is that she had little capacity for personal friendship. She was comfortable only when in the company of her immediate family. They protected her, like a stockade, from the great Beyond. I could count the number of her friends on the fingers of one hand, and later in life even they fell away. I do not remember the names of any of them – such was their impact upon my life. Such was the extent to which my mother's friends and I engaged with each other. Who was to blame for this? My mother? Myself? The friends? The fact is that she lacked generosity of spirit. She could not reach out. Nor was she well educated or widely read. Her opinions, when they were uttered at all, were rash burstings out, the stuff of cliché.

I am reminded of these sad facts by a statement in a notebook which dates from 1969, my second year at university. Amongst many fragments of poems, references to books to be read, and much blank space, I have found this: 'Here is where it starts, at the mouth – an inability to apply a word, to use it, to see it drop easily away as would a leaf, and to know that failure as the key to an impotence of self...'

The easy letting fall of a word. Ah, how marvellous that would be! Throughout my life, and like my mother before me, I have found it difficult to talk to others. As a child, I was a stammerer, and I hesitated to speak for that reason. I did not wish to make a spectacle of myself. By the time I went to university, I had become extremely guarded, fearful of showing ignorance. I felt that I lacked intelligent opinions on matters of the world. It was not only that. I could never speak fast enough. I would hone phrases inside myself, but by the time they were ready to be uttered, the moment was past and I had been left behind. Books were my consolation. A good book was a superior form of company. It was better than talk, which was random, rude and haphazard by comparison. If a book bored or disappointed, it could be tossed aside. Great books spoke with such eloquence that words uttered in the street seemed second-rate and of little consequence by comparison. So my silence, in part, was self-imposed, a decision not to speak because so few would talk back who would be worth listening to. Call that the shocking arrogance of youth. It is an arrogance that has, in part, persisted.

Dorothy Collects Her Pension at Totley Rise

Make it as far as the shops if you can, mum.
No one'll stop you.
Fiddle with your purse at the greengrocer's.
Smile weakly at the delivery man.

When you reach the post office,
Listen closely when she asks after your health.
You'll hear a word or two.
Then slide the money, in a cellophane bag,
Away from her kindly hand.

Back at your own kitchen,
You'll count it all out again with the curtains drawn,
As you always do,
The pence, the florins, the old soiled notes.
Under the bed it will go, under the floor boards.

Then you'll attend to a clatter of saucepans,
And, after a dab or two to remove the gravy
From the corners of your mouth,
A long, slow afternoon
Will be stretching ahead of you,
With a window to be watching out from.
And a good bit of sighing to be done.

Saying Goodbye to Mother in the Northern General Hospital

The last breath is the only breath.
There beside you. A small flurry of the fingers.
The last smile is the only smile.
Shawls heaped about your shoulders.

The last word is the only word.
Look after yoursen, love. Get enough to eat.
Dying away. The long, last walk.
There's loads of food in t' freezer.

The last look is the only look.
So shrunken-small beneath the blankets.
Larger than life through the eyes of a child.
Small. Smaller. Nothing.

Local Heroes: Tony Dale

Religion sucked me in at the age of thirteen. I answered the call of Jesus one rainy summer evening in a blustery marquee on the Isle of Anglesey. I became a very serious-minded Christian for about four years. Then it left me, almost as quickly as it had come. I could no longer believe the dogma. Other voices and other vices took possession of me, literary ones who believed religion to be a brazen lie: Jean Paul-Sartre and Albert Camus, for example. I began to construct an alternative deity out of despair and the richness of solitude. I was staring into the void.

As a young evangelical Christian, I was expected to join a local church. It would be good for that church if I did so, my evangelical friends advised me. I would leaven the whole. I might even persuade church-goers to accept Jesus into their hearts as their personal saviour. Church goers were viewed with a great deal of suspicion by evangelical christians. Such people believed that they were doing the right thing by God. Not so. The fact that they were so smug and so self-satisfied about their church-going meant that they were probably further away from Jesus than the most hardened sinner. So I joined the local church in order to inveigle myself, in order to do them some good. Such was the nature of my own smug teenage arrogance

That church was Trinity Fir Vale Methodist Church in Fir Vale, whose spire had been dominating the local area since 1902. The fading presence of Methodism was everywhere in north Sheffield. You saw them, often, on street corners, tiny, long abandoned chapels that had once belonged to one God-fearing Methodist sect or another. As you walked down Owler Lane towards Gregorys the baker, for example, you could see the remains of a long-disused chapel trapped within a sealed off plot of land which now held an electricity sub-station. God had lost his spark.

Trinity was a little different. It was alive. It had a modest congregation. It had its own flourishing Sunday School of which, in due course, I would become School Captain. What is more, some of its Christians were very unusual, quite unlike any others I had known.

Tony Dale, who lived with his parents in Popple Street, and worked as a technical illustrator in the steel industry, was a local preacher in the Methodist Church, which meant that he moved from church to church as the rota dictated. But did Tony really ever preach? Yes, without a doubt. And yet he never had the over-serious demeanour of a preacher. He wore jeans and roll-neck sweaters. Was he not too relaxed, too casually familiar? He was unlike any other Christian that I had ever come across. We never talked about personal salvation. His relationship with God seemed both perfectly assured and yet more distant. He was humorous, sceptical, generous. He looked a little odd. His eyes were filmy and strangely bulbous. His hair spiked forward at the front as if fashioned from tough wire, his eyelashes too. His laughter, which always seemed to come from deep in the back of his throat, seemed carelessly all-encompassing, as if he were always laughing at life's absurdities too, no matter what local incident might have prompted the laughter.

I used to puzzle over the fact that he seemed to have a near perfect set of even, false teeth – at such a young age too! What had happened to the originals? Had he ruined them by eating even more sweets than me? I never asked him that question. Falsies were usually the preserve of older people though such as my mother and grandparents. My grandfather Harold used to drop his into a thick tumbler of cold water before he went to bed, the same tumbler, as it happens, that he would drink a glass of hot water from late at night because it did him a power of good, he always used to say when challenged about the habit. When he dropped the teeth in, the water was crystal clear. By morning, I used to notice that it had gone cloudy.

False teeth in general were rather worrying. When my grandparents walked around the kitchen without their teeth in late at night, they would look unusually troubling to me – older, anxious, fearful, and even a bit helpless. Their talk would come out oddly too, as if they were chewing on their words rather than spitting them out. And that strange O shape of their toothless mouths was always such a desolate space to stare into. It made me think of dying.

And yet false teeth were perfectly acceptable, if not downright respectable, in those days. People used to say that they were less of a bother than the real things, which were forever causing aches and pains. Folks in Fir Vale, I used to think, were almost in a hurry to have their own teeth extracted.

Tony Dale entertained brazenly unorthodox ideas, tossing them around like coins. He peppered his conversation with scientific theory, Roman history, geology, references to the fourth dimension, mish-mashings of theology, Ouspensky and

Einstein, which both exhilarated and baffled me. His thoughts were forever revolving around ideas of the boundlessness of space and time. In short, he was something of a self-taught intellectual. He introduced me to the philosophy of Henri Bergson. His fascinatingly wayward and free-flowing thinking began to make evangelicalism seem curiously parochial and inward-looking. God was always deep inside there somewhere, but He seemed to be just one aspect of the marvellousness of everything else that made up the clutter and the teem of the universe. God was the softly spoken prime mover of a boundless family of forever zizzing particles. That is how Tony might have expressed it to me had I ever asked him. I never did. I merely listened, slightly awe-struck, and pondered on his elusive words.

Tony wrote a single book in his lifetime, which he published himself. It was a collection of poems called *Thursday on Manterfields Clock*, and he illustrated it with his fine and meticulous line drawings. On the title page he described himself as Anthony Dale. That use of his full name struck me at the time as a rare and uncharacteristic flourish of self-importance. He was only ever Tony to me.

He was a talented, self-taught musician who moved from instrument to instrument with extraordinary ease. When I first met him, he was playing show tunes on an old upright piano in an echoing schoolroom, without sheet music, with a kind of casual ease. Then he bought a Framus twelve-string guitar, which I coveted. He sold it to me for £9, and bought himself a set of vibraphones, which he began to play, once more with seeming ease, almost immediately.

In short, he was his own man. He bought a handsome, bay-windowed house on Barnsley Road, a third of the way up the hill towards Firs Hill School, and paid for it in cash. It cost £1,800. I often visited that house. It was echoey and very sparsely furnished, with an untended garden. I recall a teak bookcase, a Hi-Fi, a black settee, and many cups of instant coffee. Little else. It never felt much lived in. In fact, it felt like the house of a restless man who would always be passing through, always be on his way to somewhere else. In the mind, that is. That was Tony Dale. And yet he did not go far, geographically speaking. He kept his free-spiritedness and his waywardness local.

On Not Being Francisco

Jamia Mosque Ghausia and Trinity Firvale Methodist church

This mosque on Firth Park Road in north-east Sheffield has come about as a result of a strange and delicate grafting process. It is attached to the back of an imposing Christian church (see below) whose spire has commanded a view of the shops of Fir Vale since it was built in 1902. That church is still in use, though its congregation is much depleted. I see by the sign on the wall that it continues to have a Boys' Brigade too – but only just. It is much less popular than the mosque as a place of worship. What is more, most of the congregation live in other parts of Sheffield. They return there for reasons of loyalty to a near vanished community. As do I today, wandering serendipitously the streets that I knew so well as a child, a kind of curious, affable ghost, wishing to see for myself all that has gone and all that still endures. (*Post-script: Another surprise finds me emotionally unprepared this evening, even as I sit here re-reading my own words of the recent past. The Sheffield Star announces that Trinity Firvale Methodist Church is about to close its doors for the last time. It is too costly to keep up. The congregation has dwindled away to almost nothing. The Christian God will have to find a home elsewhere.)*

The minaret of the mosque, which was built in the 1980s, is entirely new. Much of the rest of the building – see the shape of its windows – were once the Sunday School rooms of Trinity Firvale Methodist Church whose back entrance – which is now the Ladies Entrance to the mosque – is on Owler Lane. You could once pass from church to schoolroom with relative ease. Now that movement – were it possible – would be from one great, world-encompassing religion to another. In fact, Fir Vale itself is predominantly Asian now, and its devout are predominantly Muslim.

I knew that church well. I was its Sunday School Captain during one of my four or so years of strict respectability, commendable dutifulness, good behaviour and religious observance – from approximately fifteen to eighteen years of age. I played Bob Dylan's 'With God on our Side', to the accompaniment of my twelve-string guitar, in my Sunday School class. I re-arranged Christina Rossetti's 'In the Bleak Midwinter', that lovely carol which she wrote in 1870 in response to a call from *Scribner's Magazine* to write a Christmas poem. In 1967 I sang my own slow and sultry version of Rossetti's words, as if re-mixed in the mind of Bob Dylan himself, to guitar accompaniment, during an evening service. Though well received, it represented, I felt, a dangerous incursion of modernity. That particular variety of modernity vanished long ago.

The businesses just beyond the church door are all gone too, of course – Gabbitas's the newsagent where I would buy my weekly copy of *The Wonder World of Do You Know*, Sockett's for all your electrical needs, Banners the haberdashery for mother's rolls of bias binding, Mr Brown's eye-catching toy shop for the newest of the Matchbox range in miniature cars and trucks, and the jewellers, which also sold a few long-playing records, including a boxed set of Churchill's wartime speeches, which I would ask to listen to, enthralled, as child.

What has not gone from these parts are the contours of the land, the precipitous risings and the sudden fallings away, the steep, twisty declivities, the pockets of old woodland, the remnants of ancient, handsome stone – some even dry-stone – boundary walls. There is so little flatness here. Streets fall away downhill as if on a childish impulse or, at Page Hall, make a sudden uphill turn, enabling me to spot, all of a sudden, the ruined shell of the building that once housed the Roxy cinema where Elvis pouted all the way through *Kissin' Cousins* in 1964. Look up and you are more often than not likely to see vistas – tree-topped hills marking the fact of a local park (one of so many) or, most majestic of all, Wincobank Hill that overlooks the once sooty industrial might of the Don Valley. Wincobank Hill, a few prefabs clinging to its south-western slope, a few dwarf oaks here and there, forever gasping for clean air, was once as brown and as tawny as some dusty lion's pelt. It is now as bushy and tree-thronged as any mountain in the Catskills. Though buildings may often look shabby and down at heel, nature still stands proud in these parts. Where a building gives up the ghost, a tree fights for the right to breathe. God be praised for the Clean Air Acts, which gradually brought about this mighty transformation.

Were my young mother still alive in the late 1950s, and I beside her looking up into her face, I would tell her that it is no longer necessary to stare out of the kitchen window apprehensively, and then rush out of doors to tear the white flannelette bed sheets from the line. The black snow of soot is no longer falling from the air, mother. Linger over your cuppa.

I am now standing in the valley's bottom, at the beating heart of Fir Vale proper, where three roads – Herries Road, Barnsley Road and Page Hall Road – meet. Directly opposite me is the entrance to a mighty leviathan called the Northern

General Hospital which seems to grow and grow even as you stare at it. Its stone gate posts are a remnant of the old Fir Vale Infirmary, I notice. Remnants of the past get pressed into service. I walk in the direction of Barnsley Road, preparing myself, having passed the ghostly space once occupied by the Sunbeam Cinema, to make the long climb uphill towards Burngreave and Pitsmoor.

But first I glance across the road, and stare in the general direction of a tree-filled, grassy pocket of ground beside the bus stop up to Sheffield Lane Top. This patch of land, bounded by a lovely, leaning stretch of dry-stone wall, was once occupied by Fir Vale's most handsome, early-nineteenth-century cottages. Everyone admired them. From the outside. Even the Queen, when she made her slow-motion, Coronation drive through Sheffield in 1953, in the black Daimler with its fluttery flag, was said to have remarked in passing upon their picturesqueness. I knew a girl who once lived in one of those cottages. They were cursed by damp. The best you could expect if you were of the hardy sort was mild ill health. Worse, perhaps even much worse, if you were delicate. This girl was delicate, her mother once told me. Picturesque or not, they were demolished in the 1960s.

As I mount the hill, young boys, many of them in caps and ankle-length white jubbahs, run past me. Perhaps they are nearly late for prayers. How recently have you seen a Christian run to pray? I ask myself. Throwing a left, I find myself in Stair Road, yet another of Sheffield's thousands of sequestered nooks. Stair Road forms one side of a kind of square, not exactly a square, with a small, tree-lined park of sorts at its centre. I am looking out for a villa on the top side of this square which was once the Manse of the local Methodist minister. Silver-haired Rev. Vinson lived there in the early 1960s. Vinson intrigued me, always. He was no great lover of human kind, I always felt. He was too severe, too impatient by half. I see him walking, unsmiling, the streets of Fir Vale, in his black, foot-lapping priestly vestments, a severe, single man who lacked the common touch. What he loved most of all was to expound on abstruse theological matters from the pulpit to utterly bemused local audiences. He possessed a most handsome library of Christian exegesis, I recall, in a room overlooking that quiet street, where no one but he ever long lingered.

I look and look – but, alas, do not spot the manse. And so I continue my way along to the end of Stair Road, and just as I am about to turn right and plunge back downhill to Barnsley Road in the general direction of my friend Herbert Green, I see an object in the front-room window of a handsome and extraordinarily spick-and-span house whose tall, peaking windows give it a decided ecclesiastical air. And, as if to emphasise that fact, there is this object of sheer fascination in the window, a crucifix. And it is by no means an unadorned Protestant crucifix. Nothing as plain, humble and self-effacing as that. Christ, in loin cloth only, hangs, head bowed, from the cross. Is this a Catholic establishment I ask myself?

I have now been pausing for so long beside the house's garden wall that a man, who has noticed my stare, comes to the door, opens it, and begins to walk down his path in my direction. He shouts something to me – or at me – which I do not hear. What kind of a response has my harmless curiosity provoked? We are almost upon each other. Then he asks me again: 'Are you Francisco?' he says. I apologise, immediately, for not being Francisco, and I tell him that I had stopped here to look because I had seen the visual witness of the crucifix pendant in his window, which struck me as an unusual sight in an area which was now predominantly Muslim. He smiles again, and tells me that there is a very active Christian community in Sheffield too. He himself is a musician at the Catholic Cathedral in the city centre. As we part, warmly, I ponder on the possibility that I might after all be a wandering, footloose christian pilgrim by the name of Francisco, seeking for meaning in a godless world, and much later to be venerated by the name of St Francis for my piety and my unusual degree of fondness for stray cats.

Hymning

> Forth in Thy name, o Lord, I go,
> My daily labour to pursue,
> Thee, only Thee, resolved to know
> In all I think, or speak, or do.
>
> *Charles Wesley, 1707–88*

The pews, as I experienced them on my backside at Trinity Fir Vale Methodist Church, were fashioned from well polished hard wood, and they kept you bolt upright, as if screwed into position. They seemed to demand: pay attention. You are here to listen, learn, contemplate, pray. This is not the saggy settee in front of the television in your cold, damp front room in Coningsby Road. This is not light entertainment of any variety. It is not Saturday night with the Billy Cotton Band Show. There will be no impromptu bursts of audience hilarity, no wild waving of Billy's baton, no clashing of cymbals, no rude rasps from an errant trombone. God is holding you to account for your presence here. God himself is making that wakey wakey call this evening. Do not disappoint him.

Every week I would sit on the back row with two or three others to left and to right of me, overlooked by the overhanging balcony, and dutifully count the numbers at Sunday evening service. In my head, of course. Occasionally I would have to bob and weave a little – as inconspicuously as possible, of course – in order to be quite sure that I had not missed anyone. A few were inclined to sit on their own, and might be part-concealed by a pillar. It was a large church, created, I always felt, for larger and more fervent local congregations than this one. We were a ragged remnant. Even the way we chose to group ourselves in that church, clusters here and there, at back, middle and front, spoke of divisiveness – or, at best, a lack of cohesiveness. We were no longer a significant cohort belonging to that great army of the saved, marching together, ever onward, to victory. We had fallen away in the recent decades. Those who had opened this church in 1902 would frown upon us for our falling away, our shameful lack of witness. That too made me feel sad, that we were so few, week in, week out, and that our predecessors had done better. On the other hand, this counting, though a mite obsessive, was something that I just had to do.

It was a tiny branch line of my obsession with such things as mental arithmetic – I liked nothing better than to beat the greengrocer to the grand total when it came to totting up the bill for fruit and veg. I had also developed a passion for numbering each letter of the alphabet, from one to twenty-six. M was dead centre, unlucky thirteen, for example; T was the perfectly satisfying twentieth letter.

If the congregation was small, I would feel sad, frustrated, disappointed. If there were more than I might ever have expected – let us say sixty for the sake of argument – I would feel stronger within myself, exhilarated, even a little puffed up – and also slightly perplexed. (Who had brought these new strangers here? Would they be here on another occasion? Could we depend upon them?) I would feel that we were marching forward as a body, making some impact upon that chilly world of godlessness (when I think back, it is almost always on a cold, dark autumn or winter evening, and never in summer that I imagine myself once again worshipping there, with the congregation a tiny marooned band of forth-shining light) just beyond the church door. Such was the wisdom of a pious teenager in a sports jacket on the very back pew.

He glances across at the list of hymns on the board at the front of the church, a list of numbers, to be read from top to bottom. He opens The Methodist Hymn Book. He opens his mouth in common with all the rest. Hymning was a pleasure...

I pause to open my old black *Methodist Hymn Book*, and I read these words, in blue biro, in my own hand. On the left-hand page I have written: ALL ONE IN CHRIST JESUS, and on the right TRINITY FIR VALE METHODIST CHURCH (double-underlined), and, beside those words, my name, address, and the date of the book's purchase: 8. 3. 65. I then turn to the Preface, which begins with these words. 'Methodism was born in song. Charles Wesley wrote the first hymns of the Evangelical Revival during the great Whitsuntide of 1738 when his brother and he were 'filled with the spirit,' and from that time onwards the Methodists have never ceased to sing.'

And so it was at Trinity Fir Vale Methodist Church in 1965. I would sing heartily during those years when I believed that Jesus was my Saviour. I knew that He would be listening to me, leaning down from heaven like a choirmaster dandling his tuning fork, judging keenly, as only he knew how, the quality and the fervour of my performance. Life was always a test. No, I did not much mind that. He was not a faceless judge. He was my friend, the greatest and most faithful friend that I would ever have. It is good to be judged by the highest standards, I always told myself, much better than to be praised or condemned by the world's godless. Their opinions counted for precisely nothing.

After I had lost my faith, I stopped singing hymns at all. As an atheist, I could not bear to go through the motions of believing – for that is what the singing of those words signified to me – when I no longer in fact believed. It would be hypocrisy, and even a kind self-perjury. I am not amongst those who sing hymns for the pleasurably, upliftingly tuneful familiarity of it all.

As I sang in those days, I would listen out for the different threads of sound: the soaring and the shrieking highs, the booming lows, and the careful in-betweens. Some of the higher threads were strange, uncertain female waverings, thin shudderings of wispily approximate fragments of notes – a little like a small, wind-buffeted light aircraft, trying to come in to land at a small, provincial airstrip on the outside of town through a swirl of thick fog. Sometimes I would sing out amongst the best, giving it my all. At other times I would hold back, merely mouthing the words in my distraction. I would spend time judging the quality of the words used – hymns by the Wesley brothers, John and Charles, and other eighteenth century masters, usually passed muster, and so I would sing them with relish. As we fast-forward towards the insecurities of the twentieth century, the quality declines, quite dramatically. I would wince at badly expressed turns of phrase, broad-brush sentimental hog-washings, moments when the writer had strained after a rhyme and fallen flat on his face into the mud of groaning cliché.

The exercise itself was, of course, a form of collective worship, a great coming together of united voices. Notionally so at least. I heard other things in that singing. I heard desperate, barely united cries of self-consolation – there were so few here to be singing their hearts out! I also felt that so many of those singing here loved singing the hymns that they knew, and that this singing was no different from the singing of any other song. It was a lovely, familiar groove into which they slipped, Sunday after Sunday. Why condemn them for this? As an evangelical Christian, a kind of over-zealous spy in their midst, I was wary of the easy habits of church goers, those who were happy to go through the motions of crooning like cats in the street and little else. As a boy of sixteen, I was an extremely severe taskmaster.

Everything Must Change – a song

The school's a Muslim temple now.
Hussain has bought the bathroom suite.
Nothing else has changed.

Korans are in the grocer's shop.
Mercedes-Benz have opened up.
Nothing else has changed.

Firth Vickers' Works on Savile Street
Have shut up shop,
The ghosts are beating
On the padlocked doors,

No work any more,
Nothing else has changed,
              Everything must change.

Herbert Green has left his bedroom: the absence of a local hero

Herbert's room

I was mildly suspicious of Herbert Green, the son of a local postman, as one would be of any potential rival in Stanley Cook's A-Level English group in the upper sixth form at Firth Park Grammar School. I recognised early on that there were only two members of that group whose opinions and gifts counted for anything, and he was the other one.

He lived – and still lives – in a semi-detached house on Barnsley Road, up the hill from Coningsby Road in the direction of Firs Hill School, which I attended from the ages of four to ten. His house was just a few doors down from The Sportsman, a pub we both frequented as teenage intellectuals, eager to drink pints of Tetley's bitter with our intellectual friends as we exchanged views about black holes and anti-matter. The fact that Herbert's home was a semi-detached house with a bit of cheekily exposed timbering, built earlier in the twentieth century, meant that he might just be – I wasn't quite sure on this point – a cut or two above us socially. His mother wasn't even born in Sheffield. She came from somewhere in the south of England, and she was what my mother would describe as well spoken – which means that she didn't speak with a Sheffield accent, not at all. My mother liked the idea of people who were well spoken – that's why she sent my sister off to her hated elocution lessons on Page Hall Road – though she wouldn't have been very happy, or felt very comfortable, talking to any of them. Bert was well – and softly, even velvety – spoken too, though there was a bit of the Sheffield accent mingled with his well-spokenness.

You will have noticed something odd about the photograph that appears at the head of this chapter. This is Herbert's room, at the back of his house, overlooking the garden. Herbert himself is absent from it, though it looks as though he has been lying on his single bed until moments ago. That bed is in a mild state of disarray. See the impression of his head in the pillow. The fact is that he has just gone downstairs to make us both a cup of tea. He refused to be photographed. What is more, he refused to allow me to use his real name. Herbert is not his real name, of course. It is the name that he has chosen to go by for the sake of this book. It is the screen that he has chosen to erect between himself and your prying eyes. He wants to put a distance between himself and this over-brief account of our friendship. He wants to be at one remove from it all. That is Herbert's style, to be removed, always, in a mild-mannered way, both absent and present simultaneously. He was due to be present at a talk about my memoir yesterday, but he was in fact absent. He had come close. He had taken a long circuitous walk in the general direction of the library, looping over past Longley Park and the site of our old school, then he had veered off, and returned home. The thought of confronting a mass of people had overwhelmed him. Today things are a little better, he tells me. Today he is wearing a temporary head, and that has helped considerably.

In the absence of Herbert himself, let me tell you a few things about this room in which he spends so much of his time. His blue house slippers are absent from it because he is wearing them, as are his green padded sleeveless jacket and his slightly marked black trousers for the same reason. A record is playing, orchestral music by Vaughn Williams. All very soothing, mild-mannered and bucolic. Beside me, on the floor in a box next to the window, are some books, displayed spines upward. Bert does not own many books these days. Little by little, he has divested himself of most of the books he ever owned. He probably feels less encumbered with fewer books. He reads less now, and the books that he tends to read are the ones he has read before. The books that I spot beside me on the floor include Rainer Maria Rilke's *Selected Poems*, a translation of the *Bhagavad Gita*, a Hindu sacred text, and a hardback copy of the *New Oxford Book of English Verse*. On the far wall just to the right of his bed head are a series of LP sleeves processing down from near ceiling height, one beneath another. I stare at an image of Frank Zappa looking dangerously, vitally moustachioed. There is also *Green Onions* by Booker T and the MGs, a sleeve of a recording of the first symphony by Elgar, and of the seventh by Vaughn Williams.

Herbert had an inimitable style as an eighteen-year-old boy at the grammar school: brown hair that bushed out wildly, like a back-combed beehive, in the manner of a famous drawing of the rebellious nineteenth-century French poet Arthur Rimbaud penned by his friend and lover Paul Verlaine, and a reserve that seemed almost unbreachable. Not that Herbert was a rebel. His rebelliousness was entirely contained within his hair, which was so shockingly different from everyone else's at Firth Park Grammar School that no one ever said a word about it. In fact, he seemed to me to be extremely mild-mannered, the very model of politeness on a social level. He never raised his voice. He never expressed revolutionary opinions. He was finically aesthetically discriminating, that's how I put it to myself as I tried to wrestle with the difficult fact of his continuing presence amongst us. He kept himself to himself, and he wrote prose about literary matters – and about poetry in particular – of such an awe-inspiring density and eloquence, long, convoluted sentences in an impeccable hand, that I was left feeling awe-struck and perhaps even thoroughly out-classed. Had I been able to fully understand his prose, I would have had a surer notion of which of us possessed the superior intellect. Obliquity is such a weapon. At least I knew for certain that he used words which utterly seduced me – sensibility, for example. Disconsolate is another. Both of them winningly and seductively polysyllabic, you will not have failed to notice.

Herbert's blind spot was examinations. He could not succeed at them. Or was it that he *would* not – *chose* not to – succeed at them? He always seemed so wilfully self-reliant. And so he failed his exams and I passed mine. Did that give me any satisfaction, that I had beaten him at that game? No, not really. In fact, I felt rather proud of him for having been so disdainful of the customary road to advancement. He had chosen to set himself apart from it. He had chosen to be his own man.

When he returns with the mugs of tea, I talk to him about the writing of this book upon which I am embarked. He is, as so often, mildly discouraging, perhaps even gently mocking in his way. Why would I want to write a patchwork of a book about local people, local places, local matters? The bookshops of Sheffield are full of books about local history. He recommends that I turn the same material into a novel, perhaps even a Lawrentian novel. That would surely widen the appeal of it. I tell him that I am writing what I am writing, that this is what I feel like being engaged in at the moment. It is sufficient unto the day. Wholly worthy of my attention or not, it is filling me to the brim. And as for there being too many books about local history, are there not also too many novels?

He sits near motionless, head hanging forward, knees and hands pressed tight together, long, gaunt face with its greying beard grazing the collar of his shirt. And why, as a part of this little project of mine, would I want to write about our friendship, he asks me? There is so little to be said, he tells me as he repeats the bald facts, which are so well known to both of us: together in the sixth form English group with Stanley Cook at Firth Park Grammar School. What else? He shrugs his bony shoulders. He seems a little thinner, a little more gaunt, every time I see him.

In short, he does not agree with me. He thinks that I am wasting myself. He thinks that I am not using my creativity. As ever, we agree to differ.

In spite of his woeful examination results, Herbert was given a place at Oxford University to read English at the end of the 1960s. They clearly saw his potential. I, on the other hand, had had to work for my place at Cambridge University. Needless to say, he did not prosper there – he was always too self-absorbed, at too oblique an angle to the world, to be at the beck and call of any of its institutions. And so, after just eighteen months he returned to Sheffield, where he worked on and off in various jobs – a hospital stores, for example – that never stretched him intellectually, but must have pleased him enough to tolerate the routine. He seldom wrote much – some verses and scraps of verses. Little else to my knowledge. I always used to feel that he was almost too fastidious ever to write. I could never imagine him writing as a miner might chip away, day in, day out, at a coal face. The circumstances were never quite propitious enough. Herbert was – and perhaps still remains – too much the aesthete. Having said that, he does have the ability to craft a good, mocking letter. What is more, he uses that gift, quite frequently, and quite unselfconsciously. He is perhaps the victim of his own acute self-consciousness.

Our friendship has remained a fast one. He views me with all the warmth allowed for by his characteristic ironic detachment, before, I imagine, turning aside in order to listen once again to Ornette Coleman's *Chappaqua Suite* in that bedroom of his overlooking the back garden, where he has brooded and dreamed life-long, amongst his dwindling store of books and CDs, about the merits and the demerits of the various differing translations of the poetry of Stéphane Mallarmé, that nineteenth-century French master of hermeticism. At least, that's how it seems.

Sheffield Trust

Having left Herbert's house, I climb the final stretch of Barnsley Road uphill towards Firs Hill School, passing the Sportsman on my way, and now I am standing at the bus stop, almost opposite the site of the Old Mojo Club, waiting for the 88 to Bents Green that will take me back into the city centre.

Suddenly I see an old, white-haired man lurching towards me propelling himself along with his stick. He has a carrier bag full of shopping in his other hand. He looks breathless. ' 'Ere y' are, love,' he says to me as he approaches. He holds out his hand, palm flat out. I step towards him, and he says to me: 'Go and get me a box of matches from that shop, will yer, love. I'm all done in. I need a rest.' He presses a fifty-pence piece into my hand, and then lurches backwards into the bus shelter where, gasping for breath, he leans back heavily against the narrow blue plastic support that passes for a seat these days. Then he pulls out a cigarette paper and begins to roll one, quite deftly, with one hand.

I run down to the shop fifty yards away – it's coming on to rain now, and the bus will be here in less than one minute – buy a box of matches from the shy young Asian boy behind the counter, run back to the old man, and press the box of matches into his hand, together with the 25 pence change. Ta, love, he says. I wink back at him as I swing onto the bus.

A Besmirched Remnant of Firth Park Grammar School

Does anything remain of Firth Park Grammar School? I find myself asking on a sunny Sunday afternoon in October as I reach the north-eastern edge of Longley Park, and stare across the road at a severely angular building, opened in 2008, which describes itself as Longley Park Sixth Form College. It trumpets its academic achievements on a banner which stirs in the wind a little beside the entrance. This school stands on the site of my old grammar school, the first such school to be built to cater for pupils in north Sheffield. Once a splendidly turreted private house owned by the Booth Family, industrialists who had once been responsible for the making of London's Southwark Bridge, floating iron girders on barges down through England's canal network, the house was sold to Sheffield Corporation by a Miss Jane Wake in October 1919, and the buildings transformed into a grammar school.

I attended the place from 1961 to 1968. The school was closed in 2002, and the building demolished in 2003. All that remains of Firth Park Grammar School now are memories, memorabilia – and a website for the sharing of reminiscences.

Is there anything at all for me to look at, even the tiniest reminder of my alma mater? I ask myself as I walk along the side of the school. Then I spot something which resonates, immediately. I recognise half of a gate post and a section of stone wall stretching away, topped by a coiling of barbed wire. This gate post and this stretch of wall are all that remain of my old school. As I step closer, levelling my camera, I see that there are some markings on the gate post. Very faint ones, in ghostly white paint, but still perfectly legible: NF. That is not quite all though. Other letters have been painted over those white letters, in green. They read SUFC. That pleases me because the meaning of that vigorous over-writing is so clear. The score line reads: Sheffield United 2, Racism 0.

Wilfred Welsby: Liverpudlian carpet layer in a cock-sure trilby

The fancy man

Toward the end of the 1960s serendipity dictated that my mother's fortunes took a turn for the better. A new man walked in through the door of 45 Coningsby Road, in a trilby set at a rather jaunty angle, carrying a Stanley knife in his trouser pocket with the keenest of keen edges. He had come to lay a carpet, and in time he found himself being offered regular cups of strong brown tea by my mother, who in my mind's eye stands there, arms crossed, beside the kitchen sink, watching him slurp the first mouthful, pinky finger stuck out, because it's piping hot.

My grandfather Harold had little time for Wilfred Welsby, the bow-legged, cheekie-chappy carpet layer from Liverpool whose practical talents dazzled all who met him. Lean and plucky as any jockey, his head would be ducked under the bonnet of a car before you had told him the name of the make. He couldn't wait to get his finger ends dirty. He could mend a stubborn, 1920s' era bakelite clock. He was faster on the draw with a Bosch drill than any man ever seen before in Coningsby Road. He had his own self-maintained caravan in Skegness. And he had the ability to charm the sheer nylons off my mother as no other man had done during my lifetime. The failure of her marriage had soured my mother against men, causing her to regard them as undependable and interested in one thing only. Except for the gods of the big screen, who could have their way with her twice a week at the Sunbeam for one shilling and sixpence a ticket from the hand of Mrs Kneeshaw at the box office.

Wilfred Welsby was no such Hollywood dream. He was bandy-legged, lean, ill-favoured, quite light of voice, with a weasily, slightly oily look, a tapering, cleft chin, and a small trilby hat that he always used to wear at an angle that he himself regarded as particularly fetching. In short, he was not beautiful, this man of small-to-medium height, but he was undoubtedly attentive, to the female kind in general and my mother in particular; and my mother, like all human beings everywhere, craved some measure of attention, someone with whom she might share the small-scale, humdrum, day-to-day monotonies of life at Coningsby Road. For, it has to be said, my mother had had little of a life to speak of since the death of her marriage – other than the delight that she took in her children. And so when the carpet layer with the cocked trilby and rather charming manner arrived one afternoon to wrestle to the ground the long fat roll of new-lay, and then taper off its edges to make it a perfect fit for the kitchen floor, and, having done that job, also seemed to have time in plenty to spare to sit back and listen to my mother's stories, and even made her laugh with a story or two of his own about working on the railways with his mates, and after all that was said and done, showed her his toil-damaged finger (she had a damaged finger too as it happens, squeezed flat by the mangle), she was more than happy to sit back on a chair by the window and listen in her turn – in spite of the fact that her own father Harold was glowering like a wronged thing, and would always glower like a wronged thing when in the presence of Wilfred Welsby – on the sofa beneath the wireless.

Having laid the carpet swiftly, deftly and cheaply, he sniffed around for other little jobs that might be needing doing, and given that my grandfather was growing a little frailer, and was no longer up to doing what he always used to do, such as flushing a door or re-glazing a window or making a new perspex windshield for his motorbike or knocking up a trolley for a child's best Christmas gift, Wilfred came in very handy thank you very much indeed, and Harold had to sullenly agree. So, from time to time, he was called back from wherever it was that he lived – Parson's Cross? (surely not there) – with his wife and dog. And then, as the friendship developed, he got into the habit of calling in, just on the off chance, without so much as an invitation, when he happened, or so he always said, to be in the area. Fortunately, he even found himself a job repairing machine tools by and by, in a small factory in Blyde Road, a street adjacent to ours, no more than fifty yards from the house. What a lucky break for one and all that was!

One small impediment to the progress of their relationship was that marriage of his, of course. It soon became evident – all these things got discussed in the kitchen in due course, over ever more frequent cups of strong tea – that he was not a happy man back home, irrespective of the fact that he was extremely attentive to his golden labrador – he carried a picture of her around with him in his wallet. She (the wife) shouted at him. She bullied and nagged him. He did everything for her. He cooked. He shopped. He cleaned. And she largely stayed at home, nursing her infirmities. What is more, he hadn't loved her for years.

A little later, we even got to see a photograph of the woman. (We'd seen the precious dog long ago). She was not a looker, we all concluded. It was a measure of his human decency that he'd stayed with her quite as long as he had, we thought privately to ourselves. She didn't make anything of her appearance, such as it was, and it wasn't much to begin with. In fact, she was hard-faced and her dress sense was quite appalling. In fact, and though it scarcely needed to be said, she was not a patch on our Dorothy herself, who had retained much of her youthful coquettishness and vivacity when called upon, and even her figure – just in case anyone other than Robert Mitchum should ever notice, we always felt. Nothing ever came easy at Coningsby Road though. For all that there was some growing mutual regard on the chairs at the front of the kitchen, the rumblings from the depths of the sofa beneath the wireless continued. The rivalry and the tug-of-war for Dorothy's affections between father and carpet-laying pretender never lessened. What is more, Harold had his own word for Wilf by and by, which was spat out at the drop of a hat: Dorothy's fancy man.

The fancy man. And, yes, quite fancy too by the standards of Coningsby Road. He had his own car, which he was perfectly capable of seeing to whenever the need arose. And, indeed, for Wilfred Welsby one of life's sweetest pleasures consisted of tucking his head beneath the opened bonnet of a car and tinkering around, oily dip stick or such like in hand, or lying full-length on the pavement, boiler-suited, with his head underneath the chassis. He earnestly believed that everyone on God's earth shared his passion for such things. In fact, he could never get that notion out of his head, no matter how often you might hint to the contrary...

So, it came to be that, with the passage of time, they could be said to be, quite unofficially though, courting, and, unsurprisingly, that caused a bit of a rumpus from the sofa at Coningsby Road and further afield too. A family rumpus was not a new thing. There was much casual talk of family estrangements when it came to Wilf's family. No, he didn't see his sister back in Liverpool, not any more, not for years, because she had made off with the money he had sent back from the war. When he returned from Burma to claim it, there was no money for the local hero to claim. So he had cut her off, and he felt nothing of it. It was all that she deserved – and more. Then there was his own son. He too had proved difficult. He too had became estranged, and remained so until death parted him from his father. According to Wilf himself, it had all blown up one Christmas Eve, when Wilf had arrived at his son's house with an armful of Christmas gifts, all wrapped up in the usual Christmas finery, for the children. Wilf had walked in the door to hand them over, brimming over with all the grandfatherly amiability of Christmas, and the next thing he knew they were being flung out onto the drive after him, like so much unwanted rubbish. So, cursing the lot of them, he left. And that was that.

After a few months of gentle, harmless dalliance, Wilf managed to rent the house next door, the very house in our back yard that had once been visited by Freddie Rafferty of Freddie and the Dreamers, dressed in his sharp cream suit as he crossed the yard to the outside lavatory. So Wilf and the ailing harridan of a wife were officially estranged at last, and the consequence of that deft manoeuvre was that the burden of seeing to the poor woman was now resting squarely upon the shoulders of the son, who, understandably enough, resented it mightily, both Wilf's walking out on his own mother, and the extra work he had to do to see to her. It was a messy situation, and Wilf left it for a life with Dorothy, his new next door neighbour, and soon his wife to be...

And Harold was unhappy about all of this, but there was nothing whatsoever that he could do about it. Dorothy had always been at his beck and call. He had always ruled the roost. Now there was another man in her life, a younger man than himself by thirty years, faster off the mark, another man for her to smile at, rather coyly, who had come accompanied by more than a passing whiff of the promise of a holiday, just for two, in a boarding house in Blackpool, driven there, with Dorothy sitting tight and pretty as an iced cake in the passenger seat, in his very own self-maintained wheels. Yes, Wilfred Welsby had a touch of modest prosperity about him. What's more, by and by, he showed off the fact, on the floor of the Tower Ballroom, Blackpool, that he could even do the two-step – and more. Wilf, in short, like him or loathe him or lump him, had become a fact of life.

The Carpet Layer from Liverpool
Courts My Mother at 45 Coningsby Road

Late in the day I think of you.
I scent your breath in my nostrils.
I touch your finger with its rings.
So many rings, from such far places.
It seemed a marvel to me then.

Late in the day I think of you.
You are with me now as we waltz the room.
Your footsteps seem so light on the linoleum.
Your voice is airily peaceful,
Sweet as this boiled sweet I am sucking on.

Late in the day I think of you.
I begin at the beginning,
With my arrival at your door.
I am a little awkward that day,
Shifting my coat from chair to chair.

You point down at the carpet.
I bring out the knife.
I pare at its edges, doing my best
To make the straightest line of my life.
And you are looking on, sweet as a peach.

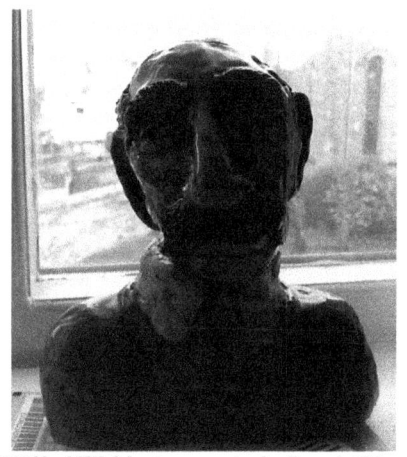

Wilfred Welsby in ceramic, by Joseph Glover

Farewell to Blackpool

Harold, me and Mabel on the prom

A new phase of my life began when I found myself rejecting Blackpool, that beloved family holiday destination of my childhood. I went there with my family for the last time in the summer of 1966, when I was seventeen years old, travelling with apprehension in the back seat of my grandfather Harold's recently purchased maroon MG Magnette Saloon, fiercely gripping the tired leather upholstery of the seat in front of me whenever my grandfather made one of his customary reckless, seize-the-moment manoeuvres with the steering wheel, and I have not returned there in nearly forty years. (By way of a short digression, I need to say that, to this day, I do not believe that the authorities acted wisely when they judged that all the various skills acquired as a result of being a life-long owner of motorbikes were quite sufficient unto the coming days of trial suffered by all who sat in the saggy passenger seats of that shabby-poshish car, of which, life-long, my grandfather was so proud.)

It was a strange coming to Blackpool that summer. I took with me six books, one for each day of the week, and a couple of spiral-bound notebooks into which I knew that I would be pouring poetical effusions. It was true. I wrote at least five poems a day, and each one was an exercise in wrestling with my strange new state of in-betweenness. I had abandoned my belief in the truth of Christian doctrine, and yet it still pulled at me, viscerally. I felt like a swimmer bravely fighting against the powerful undertow of invisible currents. I was now at least half-pledged to a new doctrine called Existentialism, which had come to me through the reading of post-war French writers, and which would grip me all the more fiercely in the coming year, when I would commit myself to an intensive period of evening study at Sheffield University. I was half the slightly craven boy and half the manly intellectual-in-the-making.

I no longer felt at home in Blackpool. I felt that it was a paradise fit only for children, and that I was no longer a child. In spite of the fact that I now regarded myself as an atheist, I wrote about Blackpool moralistically, and from a rather great and sneery height. It was all, after all, a sham. The laughter that I had enjoyed was hollow.

Laying Claim to Reality 18 August 1966

A swaying gull
agitating
its collapsible wings,
parachutes timidly
onto the summit of the Oyster Kiosk,
basking on the Promenade.
Sack-loads of trippers
gaze in awe
at Blackpool-stamped
   Hong-Kong-manufactured
imitation gold-plated bangles

    arrayed in cut-price
    shop windows.
    Headless wonders
    lay claim to reality,
    and money is shovelled
    from the dupe to the craftsman in language.
    Blackpool,
    you town of ghosts,
        and glittering facades,
    your audacity is greater than the spivs'
    who roam your
    ice-cream-wrapper-strewn,
    bingo-ticket-littered
        streets.

I would sit in a stern mood on the bench outside Mrs Ansell's boarding house in the company of Carl Jung's *Modern Man in Search of a Soul*, and look with pity at families passing by with their beach towels, brightly coloured plastic buckets and spades, and inflatable ducks. What dupes these people were! What superficial lives they had chosen for themselves.

For that, essentially, was what Existentialism was all about, the choice of one's own life. No one dictated to you what or whom you were to become. No god shaped your impulses. There was no inner voice. Everything was of your own choosing, and if you behaved otherwise, you were guilty of bad faith. In the words of a book by Jean-Paul Sartre called *Existentialism is a Humanism* which I read with an all-consuming excitement: Man is nothing else but that which he makes of himself. There is no human nature because there is no God to have a conception of it. Man simply is. I was thrilled by these words. They released me to make something new of myself. But what was that new thing to be? Would the flatlands of Cambridge tell me?

Chain-smoking with Existentialism

During my later school days, I began to study English literature with great and urgent seriousness. Why such urgency, why such an impassioned commitment? This was a moment of great emotional significance in my life. At the age of thirteen I had become an evangelical Christian, and I had cleaved to the Christian message until my final year at school. Then something tumultuous happened. I began to read more and more widely. I began to read books by authors who seemed to be at odds with everything that evangelical Christianity stood for – or who related to it in ways that caused me to question everything that I had been encouraged to believe.

I signed up for an extramural course in Existentialism at Sheffield University, given by J.P. Warrington, a member of the university's philosophy department, in the autumn of 1967. Once a week, on a Tuesday evening, I would sit at a table with a scattering of like-minded auditors (all of them older than myself) and listen to this lean-faced, chain-smoking, enormously eloquent man with a great fondness for beer as he expounded the thinking of Nietzsche, Kierkegaard, Sartre and others. I was horrified and thrilled by the dangerously searching irreverence of his words. He seemed to be challenging God head on. I felt myself to be on fire with near diabolical thoughts. Perhaps there was no deity after all. Perhaps we were all alone. Perhaps we had a duty to re-invent ourselves each new day, as Sartre suggested in *Existentialism is a Humanism*. Perhaps the next new dawn was not to be roseate after all. Perhaps it was my duty as a human being to embrace the profundities of pessimism as one might heroically choose to grasp a nettle in the hedgerow. The habitually grave and tortured look on Mr Warrington's lean face as he struggled to talk, face slightly twisted to the side, through endless upspirallings of choking cigarette smoke, seemed almost to suggest as much.

The year before, at the age of seventeen, I had found myself in the grip of a great crisis. The person I had believed myself to be was beginning to slip from my grasp. The hold of Christianity upon me, my strength and my stay for the past four years, was weakening. I was beginning to see beyond the Christian dogma that I had held to be the unshakeable truth about life. I could envisage the possibility of not being a Christian at all. Most of this debate took place inwardly. I said not a word about it to my family gathered around the kitchen table, and I knew that my fellow evangelical Christians would not be pleased to be told about my doubts. The Two Witnesses, suffused by the melodramatic ghoulishness of the stories of Edgar Allen Poe, one of my passions, was written at about this time, in September, 1966, when I was seventeen and a half years old. It is full of a terrible adolescent restlessness, a desperate, tortured over-seriousness. Who was I? What would I become? What happy-or-lucky girl would be crazy enough to want to go out with such a gloom-struck flagellant as me?

1st Witness

How long have you been passing from death to life? What force, man or God, has driven you to a realisation that you exist? I saw you this morning standing outside the gates of Christ Church, tracing a circle with your sandal in the gravel; you seemed to be waiting in anticipation of a great event. Did you discover who you really were this morning? I heard you talking to Jennifer of life after death, but do you know, are you sure, that you will be there to witness such a thing. I was walking through a garden today in my dreams, and I saw an old tombstone nearly hidden beneath the encroaching weeds: the letters engraved upon the marble were pale and faded but my memory will retain them forever. It read:

He was born in 1949, and grew up in a suburb of Sheffield: he was converted to Christianity in 1963, but it was not until 1966 that he knew that he lived, and that he was travelling – travelling with the speed of a tornado – towards something. He spent his life carrying a torch, probing into the thoughts of the world, looking for life, and now he lies, still and cold under this stone. Was he, the man, ever satisfied? He claimed to know, he claimed that he loved others – he said that he loved a nurse, but did he ever really find his life? Yes, that was the man, and that was how he lived.

2nd Witness.

I too can understand his fears for I have witnessed my own existence. I never really believed in a god of any kind – I was content to sit under the sun and file my nails, and there remains little of my time to be spent. Marx intrigued me, and I must admit that Kant's portrait hangs, adored, upon my wall, but there always was an empty chair within my house, and often I have gazed upon that chair, its varnish shimmering in the firelight, and wondered, just wondered, if, when that chair was filled, I would have found the missing link, and be able to grin triumphantly, repeating 'Life is elementary, my dear Watson.'

1st and 2nd witnesses together

We are here to ask you, plead with you to seek; to seek for a meaning for yourself. Life is futile if you must gaze upon an empty chair. There is a meaning for you. There is a path for you to tread. You must be a cog in the great machine of time, which is running down to its close, and we want you to strive, even if you die, or squander all in the process, to find life for yourself.

But where was that life to be found? Here is a note about a local walk with Tony Dale in which those baleful agonisings continue...

Tony and I went a walk together up Wincobank Hill. Starting from the prefabs which are in the process of being vacated, and stand bare, their rooms gaping obscenely in silence onto the off-white concrete road, we picked through the tufts of grass and careless small rocks, through the low-lying bushes, having to jump aside as a track motor cycle came in a thundering splutter, winding down the uneven track. Having arrived at the plateau we stopped and gazed at the landscape, a sweeping semi-circle which was spread below, minute buses crawling up the lower slopes, yellow lights flickering, outlining the trail of road and the spires and steeples, black with grime in their conspicuous arrogance, throwing themselves above the dull clamour of the corporation streets. Here we felt, was life, but such an inconspicuous mass, impersonal clusterings, where every individual had a word to say, a contribution to make, but whose voice had died away even before it had reached his own backyard gate. As we continued on our way towards the now-deserted gun turrets which crested the hill, superfluous monuments, we discussed freedom and pre-destination, I arguing that man is what his environment has made him and nothing more, that free will is nonexistent since the choice in a sense has already been made by the influences that have acted upon him up to the moment of the taking of the decision. A man may have 'realized' as a result of the teaching which has been given to him and the personal experiences which have resulted from the following of such teaching, that he must break away from the banality of a day-to-day existence, and devote himself to this new freedom which he has discovered, teaching others to walk in the same path as he, since this will also be their freedom, however, he is not free at all, he has merely followed the dictates of his new environment and rather he has entirely conformed to these principles which he has recently learnt, though they may be entirely different to his home background. Man is too afraid to contemplate real freedom, since it would involve selfishness, which, in effect, is the only real denial of self, since it leads to disintegration of character. This freedom, terrible to contemplate, is the only true freedom: that which dares to experience the basest emotions, lives most monotonously, lies most deceitfully.

Our speech was drowned by the glow of fluorescent lights and the footsteps upon the pavement as we approached Fir Vale once again. Now we understood our imprisonment, the eternal imprisonment, which we had called freedom, yet the air now was none the less fresher than it had been in the early evening...

My faith fell away almost as quickly as it had come. The dogmas of the Christian Church no longer seemed credible. When that happened, a huge emotional void opened up inside me. What would I fill it with?

The Start of a New Life

When my Uncle Ken and Auntie Ena drove me down to Cambridge to begin my new life at the university there in the autumn of 1968, they were both highly respectable people in early middle age, much more respectable than my own mother, Dorothy. They were also less eye-catching, less raucous, less fiery, less unpredictable than my mother. My Aunt Ena would not have hung out her knickers from the clothes line in the back yard. My Aunt Ena would not have greedily sucked on her finger ends after tweaking a sausage out of a sizzling frying pan. My Aunt Ena would never have strip-washed at the sink or left her pillow slip unchanged for weeks on end until it turned grey with grime. In short, my Aunt Ena, I believe, regarded my mother as somewhat uncouth and just a little beneath her, socially. Unsurprisingly, they never greatly liked each other.

My uncle married my aunt on 29 May, 1965 when I was sixteen years old. Until then we had grown up together, father and son in all but name, in that small terraced house in Coningsby Road, Fir Vale, with various other relatives, including a sister and my mother's parents, Mabel and Harold Hickson. Six people, several of them quite loud and opinionated, pressed into a small house. In Ken's final years at home, we had shared the small front bedroom which overlooked our asphalted back yard and its unpromising, unyielding rockery with a single, sooty laburnum tree. That bedroom was just large enough for two single beds, with space enough – just – to pass sideways between them. My uncle kept a chamber pot underneath his bed into which he would riddle from time to time, standing stock still, very discreetly, in the dark of night, without ever saying a word. I said nothing either. I cocked an ear instead. A significant amount of time always passed between his standing upright and that sound of urination – he was a tall man, my uncle. I rather liked that sound of gentle tinkling.

Ken and Ena had got to know each other as I grew towards maturity. They shared certain passions – tennis, hiking, nights out at the Sheffield Playhouse, Gilbert and Sullivan, the symphonies of Beethoven, and participating in amateur theatricals. Ken was a box office manager of sorts – but only in the evenings. During the day, when his prospects were not blighted by bouts of unemployment, he worked as a book keeper, an occupation which sounds better when known by the alternative name of accountant. He was always known as an accountant in later life. When they married, Ken left Fir Vale forever, and he began to change into a slightly different kind of a person, more respectable, more reserved, more cultured perhaps. He moved into Ena's flat in Broomhill, a much more respectable part of town to the South-West of Sheffield's city centre, where the soot from the steel works never fell, a part of town quite close to Sheffield University, a part of town prettified and aggrandised by the city's Botanical Gardens, boasting handsome stone-clad houses of generous proportions, part-hidden behind sheer stone walls, which seemed to yearn in the general direction of Derbyshire and the wholesome air of the Peak District.

Ah, respectability. Did they escort me to Cambridge University in my uncle's Morris Minor for this reason? Did they generally regard themselves as the acceptable face of my family? True or not, there were certain small rituals to be observed when they were with me in Cambridge. Those visits to the Turk's Head in Trinity Street, for example. The Turk's Head was what you might now call a bistro. If you sat at the table in the window, you could just about see the grand gatehouse of Trinity College. It was a restaurant with a limited menu – my choice would always be the same: gammon and chips – but a certain modest hauteur. Any restaurant would have seemed like that to me in those days. The restaurant experience was something that I had never enjoyed as a child – unless you count the occasional visit to a fish and chip restaurant during that blissful summer-holiday week in Blackpool. Where were the restaurants in Sheffield anyway? I cannot name a single one. The eating-out habits of my early life consisted almost entirely of bringing battered cod and chips in, wrapped in sheets of the *Green 'Un*, our local sports paper, from the Sunbeam Fish Bar at the end of Coningsby Road, and then of spilling the whole lot out onto a dinner plate, dousing them with malt vinegar, sprinkling them with salt, and then eating them at the kitchen table to the accompaniment of thin rounds of heavily marged – Stork – sliced white bread and a steaming hot cup of Tetley's tea. That kind of marvellous spread – my mouth waters all over again at the very thought of it – was especially to be recommended after two or three pints of best bitter at the Sportsman on Herries Road. I used to collect the fish and chips on the way back home. It was downhill, head gently swimming, all the way. There was always a lot of light and a lot of banter and a great deal of noise of crozzling chips at the Sunbeam Fish Bar.

By distinction, there was very little talk at our table in the Turk's Head on Trinity Street. My uncle was a slow and finicky eater who tended rather to pick at his food, adjusting, and then re-adjusting, its position on the plate. Much of his time was spent looking at it, appraising its potential as a near-immediate source of pleasure. In fact, there was very little talk whenever my family sat around a table to share a meal, no matter how humdrum or elevated the location. Why talk when you were intent upon eating? Why let good food cool on the plate when it could be eaten piping hot as the cook had surely intended? All that seemed to make perfect good sense to me. The idea that you might use dining out with others as an occasion to talk at length to other people at the table, to engage in the kind of competitive word-sparring which was clearly designed to impress and outface other diners, was something of which I only became aware when I began to accept, with great and grudging unwillingness, invitations to eat out in Cambridge with my college tutors.

Neil Armstrong, The Future and I: a conclusion

I had stepped onto that pavement in Cambridge in the autumn of 1968 with no small measure of trepidation. Truth be known, I felt a little lighter than air because nothing had yet happened to persuade me that I had not in fact landed in paradise. Alas, Cambridge was not the paradise that I had imagined I to me, but that is a story for another time.

Nine months or so later, Neil Armstrong would ease himself down from his landing craft onto the surface of the moon. I would watch those first shuffly-sliding, historic steps of his on a flickering, black-and-white screen in the front room of my home at 45 Coningsby Road, Sheffield 5, to the accompaniment of the welcoming, warming fizz of the newly installed gas fire. What Neil Armstrong and Buzz Aldrin did on that historic day had a profound effect upon the way I lived my own life, I believe. That first step on the moon seemed to suggest that the future was about proceeding ever onward and upward, eyes forward, never looking back.

Forty years later I paused in that ever onward and upward trajectory, and then began to look back.

Epilogue
How These Memoirs Came to be Written

It is possible to bury your childhood and early manhood until relatively late in the day. I have done it for most of my life. What finally caused me to look back was a question that my nephew put to me about seven years ago. Had I written any poems about Sheffield? he asked. He was preparing for publication a book called *A Sheffield Miscellany*, and he wondered whether I had written anything that might be a possible contender for inclusion. I began to rummage amongst my papers, intrigued by his question. I discovered that I had written a few, but it was a very few. One or two of them had even been published in my first full-length book, *Impossible Horizons*, in 1995. Why had I not written more though? I wondered. It even began to trouble me that I had not written more. Why had I paid so little attention to those formative years of my life in Sheffield? I had lived in Fir Vale until the age of nineteen, and then I had gone off to university in Cambridge. After that, I had never lived in Sheffield permanently again, although I have always been a frequent visitor because my mother lived here until her death in 2009, and my three nephews still live in the city.

I have therefore been a kind of self-imposed exile of sorts for more than forty years. Not out of choice, it has to be said. The fact is that the scope for pursuing the kind of career that I craved for, that of a writer and editor, would have been almost impossible in Sheffield, and especially during those years before the web gave us the extraordinary flexibility to be in various otherwheres simultaneously. Most of the publishing companies were in London, and it was therefore to London that I had to look if I were to fulfil that ambition. I was fortunate. I got a job as a junior editor almost immediately after I graduated, and it was based in South Kensington, as I suspected it might need to be. I became a Londoner by adoption. There was no choice.

I married, became a father, moved on to other, similar jobs. The kind of life trajectory that I was following, I reflected much later, could be likened to something extraordinary that happened on 20 July, 1967. I saw the drama of that day played out on our small, black-and white television screen in the cold front room at 45 Coningsby Road. Neil Armstrong took those first few tentative steps across the surface of the moon. It seemed like a miracle of sorts. It also presented itself to me, I believe, as a kind of model for how I might live my life. That journey towards the moon was ever onward and upward. There was no looking back. To look back would be to fail, to fall away. I believe that I had that working model for my life in my head for decades. It seemed to be in tune with how I was living my life, working as an arts journalist who is forever full to the brim with the happenings of the present – the present never stops coming, and it is the role of the good journalist to make sense of it in relation to the past. It is also his job to anticipate the future. Little of this gives much importance to looking back. Tomorrow's paper is what counts.

Then, eight years ago, and directly as a consequence of that question posed by my nephew in Sheffield, that life model changed. I took something else as my model, something locally based, something that had been an exciting part of my childhood. I am referring to what happens over at the Owlerton Speedway Track. There the bikers roar off, front wheels rising, bucking like rampaging steers, around a dirt track to the roars of the crowd and, within less than a minute, they are back to where they began. The reality is not onward and upward. It is circular. You end up where you first started, and in no time at all. This is exactly what began to happen to me as I thought and thought about what Neil had said to me.

I thought about poems at first because, aside from my journalism, I have devoted much of my writing life to poetry. I soon located the few that I had written about Sheffield, and then, quickened by my nephew's interest, and knowing also that he had been asked to help promote the regeneration of the Moor and the re-siting of the Central Markets' building, I wrote more. Much to my surprise, I even wrote a poem in praise of the great shopping street that the Moor used to be in the 1970s – that poem is in this book. A plan was then hatched to publish my next, full-length book of poetry in Sheffield, and to draw attention to its publication by displaying some of my Sheffield poems on a series of hoardings surrounding the new Markets building, together with a selection of archival photographs of my childhood and some of the places that I had known – Roe Woods, for example, that marvellous surviving fragment of 16th century woodland that had been gifted to the city by the Duke of Norfolk at the end of the nineteenth century. All that happened in the autumn of 2009.

And yet some part of me felt that still more might remain to be done. Poems tell stories – when they tell stores at all – very briefly, and they do not suit all temperaments. I gradually became aware that it might be of interest to me, and of interest to readers too, if I were able to tell the story of my growing up in Sheffield in prose. Prose issues from all our mouths, every day of the week, poetry less frequently. Would that story be of interest though? There were other issues too. Could I remember enough? Had all that happened in my life been sufficiently interesting? Had I indeed done much at all? I had never excelled as a sportsman. I had not marched across the Derbyshire fells in record time. I had not apprehended a burglar at dead of night, and marched him by the scruff of the neck to the nearest lock-up. I had not rescued a child from a house fire. I had no great tales of derring-do to recount, none whatsoever. Nor had I ever been much of a story teller. I was more of a silent brooder than a talker. In fact I seemed, when I thought about it, to have spent my life mooching around on street corners, watching other people going about their perfectly ordinary lives – rather in the way that I was getting on with mine.

What is more, how much could I actually remember about my childhood? A relative of my wife's once boasted that he could remember being born. In my mind's eye I see him rocketing, with gleeful slipperiness, out of the womb in a species of theme-park dare-devilry. Not so me. I probably crept out apprehensively, craning my neck to left and right. I had been born at home, so perhaps I was less distressed than I might have been had I been delivered in the Fir Vale Infirmary. Who knows?

That was a great fear then, my shameful ignorance of who I had been, and how I had behaved myself. There were other fears too. Even were I able to remember all that I could remember, would there ever be enough to make up what is commonly known as a book? A book sounded like such a mountain to climb. How could I fill a book with the humdrum, hole-in-corner doings of a lad born in average-to-dull circumstances in a nowhere place such as Coningsby Road? And there was a third nagging fear too. If I were to throw myself headlong into this project, what impact was that decision likely to have upon my own life and that of my family? Is it not possible that as I brooded upon the antics of my disciplinarian grandfather Harold that I would become a little like him in my turn, and that our relatively tranquil family life would suffer accordingly? Could the clamorous dead precipitate a divorce?

There were other reasons to feel anxious too. I have a dread of nostalgia, the way certain writers and filmmakers have of making the past seem so harmlessly seductive. I did not want to suggest that anything was other than it had been. I didn't want to pretend that my childhood had been a glorious, soft-focus romp courtesy of Miramax Films, a species of grittily glamorous, low-life costume drama.

So, burdened with all my fears and apprehensions, I wrote a few thousand words. Much to my surprise, they came relatively easily. What is more, I found myself able to write relatively unselfconsciously. I also found myself remembering what I had believed to be forgotten forever. I was discovering, much to my amazement and delight, that when I pushed open a door, that door opened onto another door, which in its turn opened onto yet another door. Details that I had believed lost forever came crowding in to paper the blank spaces. I showed these words to Neil. He liked them. I pressed on.

A modicum of panic ensued. I needed to find a way of dealing with the fact that I was now knowingly dedicating myself to the writing of what amounted to a full-length book. Was there any tactic I could use that would enable me to write this book without actually acknowledging the fact that it was a book at all? I thought back to a ruse that had helped me to do other exercises in extended prose writing. I would set myself a daily word count, and think no further than that. Sufficient unto the day were the troubles thereof. So I decided to write 1,000 words a day, and when that was done, to close down the computer with a huge sigh of relief. The next morning I would set myself that same task of writing 1,000 words once again, and so on. If, in the course of time, these daily gobbets of 1,000 words chose to gather themselves into what others were happy to describe as a book, so be it. I would not deny it. What is more, and more to the point, I would be perfectly happy. I would not resist such convenient labelling.

But how long would this extended subterfuge need to go on for? I knew that I simply could not bear to be in the company of my forebears for too long. It would be too oppressive and, as I have already mentioned, it could have disastrous consequences. So I decided to set an arbitrary limit for myself, a total word count, and when I had reached that limit, I would decide that the book was done. The figure that I plucked out of the air was 50,000 words. As an editor, I knew that to be the length of a short book. What is more, something else had occurred to me which helped me along my way. As I laboured during that first week, I came across, quite by chance, a helpful reference to the fact that the Nobel Prize winning Southern American novelist William Faulkner – a novelist I happened to admire a great deal – had written a masterpiece called *As I Lay Dying* in six weeks flat. I was so taken by that brief span of time. That sprint to the finishing line seemed so seductive. I pledged to do the same. I did not, however, pledge to write a masterpiece.

And so it was written, in a breathless six weeks of intensive work, in various different locations. I knew that it could not be written in Sheffield because the present would be in perpetual conflict with my memories of the past. In fact, it needed to be written a goodly distance away. And so the writing happened in three places: in a house in the country outside Carcassonne in the south of France; in my own home in South London. It was finished in a sparsely furnished spare room, iPad on my knee, in Hackensack, New Jersey. That was not quite the end, of course. Dr Johnson, the great 18th-century dictionary maker, was a very fast writer too, and he commended fast writing – if the thoughts come fast, there is no reason not to write them down as they emerge. But – but – having done so, there must then be scrupulous attention paid to what you have written at such a breakneck speed. Only some of one's first thoughts are necessarily the best ones. And so I fiddled and I tinkered and I checked and I added for about another month or so.

And then I let myself go.

About the Author

Michael Glover was born in Fir Vale, Sheffield, and was educated at Firs Hill Primary School, Firth Park Grammar School, and Queens' College, Cambridge. Poet and art critic for the *Independent*, he is also the poetry editor of the *Tablet*. As an arts journalist, he has been a regular contributor to *The Times*, the *Financial Times*, the *New Statesman* and *The Economist*. He has been a London correspondent for *ArtNews*, New York. His on-line, international poetry journal, *The Bow-Wow Shop* (www.bowwowshop.org.uk) first went online in 2009. His most recent books are: *Great Works: Encounters with Art* (Prestel, 2016), *Only So Much* (his seventh collection of poetry), *and Headlong into Pennilessness, a* memoir of growing up in Sheffield. Two collections of poetry are coming soon: *Hypothetical May Morning* and *The Book of Extremities*. His new guide book to Sheffield, *111 Places You Must not Miss in Sheffield*, will be published by Emons in December, 2017. His next book, to be published by Lund Humphries in the autumn of 2018, will be a study of the Leipzig painter Neo Rauch.

www.ingramcontent.com/pod-product-compliance
Lightning Source LLC
Chambersburg PA
CBHW040328300426
44113CB00020B/2690